LASTING
ECHOES

JOSEPH BRUCHAC

▲ ▲ ▲ ▲ ▲

LASTING ECHOES

▼ ▼ ▼ ▼ ▼

AN ORAL HISTORY
OF NATIVE AMERICAN
PEOPLE

Assemblage and painting by Paul Morin

SILVER WHISTLE

HARCOURT BRACE & COMPANY

San Diego   New York   London

For those who remember to listen

—J. B.

To Paula, for guidance along the path

—P. M.

Text copyright © 1997 by Joseph Bruchac

Illustrations copyright © 1997 by Paul Morin

Acknowledgments of permission to reprint
from previously published material appear on page 147.

Silver Whistle is a trademark of Harcourt Brace & Company.

Library of Congress Cataloging-in-Publication Data
Bruchac, Joseph, 1942–
Lasting echoes: an oral history of native American
people/Joseph Bruchac; illustrated by Paul Morin.—1st ed.
p.   cm.
"Silver Whistle."
Includes bibliographical references.
Summary: Discusses the history of Native Americans, with a
sampling of excerpts from their own accounts of their experiences.
ISBN 0-15-201327-X
1. Indians of North America—History—Juvenile literature.   2. Oral
tradition—United States—Juvenile literature.   [1. Indians of
North America—History.]   I. Morin, Paul, 1959–   ill.
II. Title.
E77.4.B77   1997
973'.00497—dc21   97-11884
Text set in Fairfield Light
Designed by Camilla Filancia
First edition   F E D C B A
Printed in the United States of America

CONTENTS

PREFACE

W HEN I WAS growing up, my formal education was filled with the traditional courses in American history. I was taught about the "founding fathers" of this country, the major battles of the Civil War, and the like. But another part of me longed to know another history, the history of my American Indian ancestors.

Parts of that history were given to me in the stories I heard—not from my own relatives, for the Indian blood on my mother's side was a family secret not to be openly discussed—but from American Indian people I met first as a child and then developed lasting friendships with as an adult.

Some of those Indian people came to my father's shop, for he was a taxidermist and sold deerskins that Native American craftspeople used. My father was a child of Slovak immigrants, but his first business partner was an American Indian taxidermist and artist named Leon Pray. Even though the Indian blood was on my mother's side, people often assumed from his looks that it was my father, not my mother, who was of Indian ancestry. Dad cherished his Indian friends. While looking through an old address book of my father's last year, I found a notation about the visit to his shop of an Onondaga woman named Alice Papineau in 1952. Three decades later, that same Onondaga elder, having become the head of the Eel Clan and one of my dearest friends and teachers, would give me an Onondaga name—Gah-ne-goh-he-yoh, "The Good Mind."

Other friends and teachers were people I met while they were working as Indians—"playing Indian" at summer tourist attractions in the Adirondacks. There was Mdawelasis/Maurice Dennis, an Abenaki basketmaker and storyteller who worked at the Enchanted Forest in Old Forge. It was Maurice who first told me that the thirteen plates on the turtle's back stood for the thirteen Abenaki nations and the American Indian concept of the thirteen moons of each year. Swift Eagle was a Pueblo Apache man who worked at a place called Frontier Town. He told me how he had been sent by his people at Santo Domingo Pueblo in New Mexico to be an ambassador to the white world, to help them see what Indians are really like. For a time he worked in Hollywood, appearing in such movies as *They Died with Their Boots On*, in which an actor named Errol Flynn played George Armstrong Custer. But his people saw some of those movies and disapproved of them, so he left Hollywood. Then there was Mohawk elder

Tehanetorens/Ray Fadden, who worked for a time at the Indian Village in Lake George. In addition to running the archery range, Ray would lecture the tourists about the contributions his Iroquois people had made to American democracy by providing a model for the American Constitution. None of the stories shared with me, first during my childhood and then when I was a young man seeking out his roots, were stories that were in any of my high school or college texts.

I began to notice at a very early age that American Indians saw history in a very different way. It was not that they were silent. From the earliest days of this country, American Indians were speaking and writing their minds. They did so with great eloquence, patience, and humor. But their voices went largely unheard, and their stories were often told by non-Indian writers in ways that were distorted or untrue.

This book brings together a sampling of some of the words I have grown to know and respect. It is an attempt to listen to the voices of American Indian people, to present what they might tell us of the history of their lives in this land. It is only a beginning, but every journey begins with the first small step.

Wlipamkaani. Travel well.

INTRODUCTION

The whole world is coming.

A nation is coming, a nation is coming,

The Eagle has brought the message to our people.

The father says so, the father says so.

Over the whole earth they are coming.

The buffalo are coming, the buffalo are coming,

The Crow has brought the message to our people.

The father says so, the father says so.

LAKOTA GHOST DANCE SONG

AMERICAN INDIANS have been telling their own stories for countless generations. Deep, varied oral traditions existed in precontact times and still exist on the North American continent. These songs and traditional stories, including epic works, could fill many volumes. They have great meaning within the individual cultures, meaning that is often not easily understood by an outsider. Even in translation and out of context, however, these oral traditions have been praised for their beauty, and are now being studied as literature. Not only have dozens of anthologies of traditional Native American poetry been published, but courses in Native American literature are regularly taught in the universities of America and Europe. The echoes of the oral traditions can be found in the words that were spoken by Indians to Europeans or set down by Indians who had mastered European traditions of writing. The graceful economy of Native American poems, such as the following three Anishinabe songs, is reminiscent of Japanese haiku:

As my eyes search the prairie
I feel the summer in the spring.

I thought it was a loon
but it was my love's canoe paddle.

Sometimes I go around pitying myself
while all the time I am carried
by the wind across the sky.

TRADITIONAL *(Anishinabe)*

Native American oral traditions may include myths and legends, tribal history, personal experience, dreams, and visions. These traditions show us a world where everything is alive and everything has a voice. One of my own favorite poems is the Abenaki "Song of the Stars," which uses the voices of the stars themselves to speak of the Milky Way (regarded as the road our spirits follow to reach the Hunting Ground in the sky after we die) and the constellation of the Big Dipper (seen by the Abenaki as a great bear pursued by three hunters).

> *We are the stars who sing.*
> *We sing with our light.*
> *We are the birds of fire,*
> *We fly over the sky.*
> *Our light is a voice.*
> *We make a road for the spirits,*
> *For the spirits to pass over.*
> *Among us are three hunters*
> *Who chase after a bear.*
> *There is never a time*
> *When they are not hunting.*
> *We look down upon the mountains.*
> *This is the song of the stars.*
>
> TRADITIONAL *(Abenaki)*

There are also long oral traditions in many Native American cultures that can only be described as epics. Among the once warring nations of the Iroquois, for example, the story of the founding of their Great League of Peace by Hiawatha and a man known as the Peacemaker takes many days to tell. The constitution of their Great League, which was created prior to the fifteenth century, is itself impressive, expressed in powerful language with logic and care. The following is from *The Law of the Great Peace.*

Five arrows shall be bound together very strong and shall represent one Nation each. As the five arrows are strongly bound, this shall symbolize the complete union of the nations. Thus are the Five Nations completely united and enfolded together, united into one head, one body, and one mind. They therefore shall labor, legislate, and council together for the interest of future generations.

TRADITIONAL *(Iroquois)*

When I listen to the voices gathered in this book, I hear many generations of our people. They speak with the voices of this land, the winds of the northern plains, the roll of waves on the Atlantic and Pacific shores, the rumble of the hooves of the vanished buffalo herds. These are the words of some of the countless Native American men and women who never forgot that their own lives and the lives of their people were one.

The history of the American continent has usually been seen through European eyes. Yet there were people here long before the coming of the Europeans, and the descendants of those original native people still remain on this land. From the first recorded contact more than five hundred years ago to the present day, the people who became known as Indians and Native Americans have described themselves and their cultures, their beliefs and their dreams. To understand what it is to be an Indian, we must listen to their voices and try to see the world through their eyes.

Native Americans are like and also unlike any other Americans. Like African Americans, Native Americans were sometimes sold as slaves. Yet the Africans were brought as slaves from across the ocean, while the native people were slaves in their own lands. Like Native Americans, the Africans came from many different tribal nations and spoke many different languages. Yet when those African slaves reached America, they were prevented from speaking their languages and maintaining their tribal identities. It has taken much effort for contemporary African Americans to learn more about the tribes and identities of their ancestors in another land. Native Americans, on the other hand, have often remained on the same land as their ancestors. About 210 original Native American tribal languages are still spoken in the United States today.

American Indians are people with many different native languages and tribal identities, who come from many different "nations." As much as Native Americans from different tribal nations have in common with each other, they also differ as much from one another as Italians differ from Swedes or Russians differ from English. There are differences in physical appearance, in dress, in traditional dwellings, and in oral traditions. Language is one way that those differences are very evident.

Not only are there hundreds of distinct Native American languages, but there are a number of different language families in North America. A language family is a group of languages that are related to one another and may have come from a common shared language in the past. In North America, American Indian language families include Hokan-Sioux, Uto-Aztecan, Athabascan, Pentutian, and Algonquian. As groups of people moved around the continent, leaving one community and starting another, they took their languages with them, often into areas where another language family already existed. Thus, in the northeast, the language of my own Abenaki people is an Algonquian language and is quite similar to the languages of the northern Cree and the Great Lakes Ojibway. Our closest neighbors to the west, the Mohawk, speak a Siouan language that is related to Cherokee and Pawnee. Abenaki is very different from Mohawk, as different as Chinese is from English. If I were to say "thank you" in Abenaki I would say *wliwini*. In Mohawk I would say *niaweh*. To say "human beings" in Abenaki I would say *alnobak*. In Mohawk I would say *ongweonweh*.

American Indian cultures are sometimes divided into such "culture areas" as the Northwest, the North, the Great Lakes, the West, the Southwest, the Great Plains, the Southeast, and the Northeastern Woodlands. The native people in each culture area survived due to a deep knowledge and a careful use of their environments. When they moved to a new area or things changed, they were quick to adapt. Just how adaptable our people have been can be seen in the way the horse was so quickly incorporated into the cultures of the Great Plains. Before the coming of the Europeans, there were no horses in North America. In the languages of the Great Plains this wonderful new animal became known as the "Spirit Dog," or the "Spirit Elk." Within two generations of the introduction of horses, the Cheyenne and Lakota, who had formerly been farmers, had moved onto the plains as buffalo hunters on horseback. "Adapt to survive" was the way of Native American cultures.

Consider the lives of such southwestern native peoples as

the Pueblo and Hopi and such northwestern nations as the Tlingit and Kwakiutl. The Pueblo and Hopi live in apartment buildings made of adobe brick. The Tlingit and Kwakiutl build longhouses out of cedar planks cut from the living trees. While the Pueblo and Hopi rely on farming the desert as the main source of their food, growing corn and beans and squash, the Tlingit and Kwakiutl turn to the ocean, fishing and hunting sea creatures from giant canoes.

Henry Rowe Schoolcraft was an Indian agent among the Ojibway in the last century. He married an Ojibway woman, and was one of the first non-native people to try to see this continent and the experience of the Native American through Indian eyes. In 1839, his (and his wife's, though she was never formally given credit) translation of Native American tales entitled *Algic Researches* was the first publication of American Indian traditional literature. Schoolcraft made these remarks in a diary entry on July 31, 1822.

> *Who would have imagined that these wandering foresters should have possessed such a resource? What have all the voyageurs and remarkers from the days of Cabot and Raleigh been about, not to have discovered this curious trait, which lifts up a curtain, as it were, upon the Indian mind, and exhibits it in an entirely new character.*
>
> HENRY ROWE SCHOOLCRAFT, 1822

How different is it to see "through Indian eyes"? Imagine this: What if European explorers had not "discovered"

America? Then the advanced civilizations of Central America, such city-states as those of the Aztec and Maya, would not have been conquered by the Spanish. Perhaps the Aztec might have become more technologically advanced than Europeans, inventing airplanes and powerful weapons a hundred years before such things were invented in Europe. What if those Aztec had then flown across the ocean and invaded Europe with the aim of turning it into an Aztec colony? Europeans would be told they had to give up their own languages and speak only Nahuatl. European wealth and property could have been taken and many people sold into slavery, while Aztec leaders debated whether or not these Europeans would be labeled as renegades and savages.

Does it all sound strange and extreme? In large part, this is how things happened on the American continent.

One of the concepts held by many of the different Native American nations is the idea of seven generations. It is said, for example, in the oldest oral traditions of the Iroquois that whenever we do something, we must do it with seven generations in mind. How will our actions affect the lives of those who live seven generations from now? In a 1990 interview, Oren Lyons, a contemporary Faith Keeper of the Onondaga nation of the Iroquois, said:

In our way of life, in our government, with every decision we make, we always keep in mind Seven Generations to come. It's our job to see that the people coming ahead, the generations still unborn, have a world no worse than ours—and hopefully better. When we walk upon

Mother Earth we always plant our feet carefully, because we know the faces of our future generations are looking up at us from beneath the ground. We never forget them.

OREN LYONS (*Onandaga*), 1990

I've had it explained to me by other Iroquois elders that the current generation must view itself as being in the middle of seven generations. We have three generations that we can remember, who came before us—our parents, our grandparents, and our great-grandparents. We have three generations who will come after us, whom we may be fortunate enough to know during our own lifetimes—our children, our grandchildren, and our great-grandchildren.

There is also a seventh-generation prophecy. Almost every native person I know has heard of this prophecy, but no one can say for sure when it was first spoken or who spoke it. Some say it was first spoken by Tecumseh in the early 1800s. Or by Crazy Horse six decades later. Or by an Anishinabe holy man who lived two generations before the coming of the Europeans. The prophecy might be said to be part of contemporary Pan-Indian oral tradition.

The prophecy says that seven generations after the coming of the Europeans there will come a time when the native people will again grow strong. That seventh generation is the generation that many Native American people say is the generation of today.

The *Tadadaho* is the principal chief of the league of the Iroquois. Tadadaho Leon Shenandoah, who passed on in July 1996, expressed his view of the seventh generation this way:

Look behind you. See your sons and your daughters. They are your future. Look farther and see your sons' and your daughters' children even unto the Seventh Generation. That's the way we were taught. Think about it: you yourself are a Seventh Generation.

LEON SHENANDOAH (*Iroquois*), 1990

The history of the American Indian is a tale still being told. Seven generations is a circle that has no end. That circle is strengthened with the breath of each new child.

LASTING
ECHOES

In the past 190 years, the U.S. Government has tried every possible way to get rid of the troublesome Indian problem he feels he has on his hands. First the Government tried extinction through destruction—where money was paid for the scalps of every dead Indian. Then the government tried mass relocation and containment through concentration—the moving of entire tribes or parts of tribes to isolated parts of the country where they were herded like animals and fed like animals for the most part. Then the government tried assimilation—where reservations were broken up into allotments (an ownership system the Indians did not understand) and Indians were forced to try to live like white men. Indian dances and Indian handwork was forbidden. A family's ration of food was cut off if anyone in the family was caught singing Indian songs or doing Indian handcraft. Children were physically beaten if they were caught speaking Indian languages. Then termination was tried by issuing forced patents in fee to Indian land owners—land was taken out of the trust relationship with the U.S. Government, and an unrestricted patent in fee was issued to the Indian whether he wanted it or not, or whether he understood it or not.

EARL OLD PERSON (Blackfeet), 1966

I. WELCOME, FRIENDS

My heart is not mine but yours;

I have no men; they are all yours;

command me in any difficult thing;

I will do it . . .

UNCAS *(Mohegan)*, 1638

IT BEGAN with welcome. Throughout the continent of North America, the place called Turtle Island by many Native Americans, the greeting in many of our indigenous languages is similar. *Hau, kola,* say the Lakota of the Great Plains. *Kwai, kwai, nidoba,* say my own Abenaki people. Both greetings mean "hello, my friend." The earliest English dictionary of a native language was composed by Roger Williams in the 1600s. It includes the Narragansett words of greeting: *What cheer, netop.* "Hello, my friend," yet again.

The first contacts between Native Americans and European settlers were often ones of friendship and sharing. The native people of the Americas appear to have always shown a willingness to welcome and even adopt outsiders. To this day, ceremonies in which we make new relatives through adoption are of deep importance to many of the more than four hundred indigenous tribal nations. Most often, adopting an unrelated person—as a son or daughter, as a father or mother or grandparent—was done within one's tribe. Yet people from other tribes were also freely adopted into the tribe itself. When the new people arrived on the shore, they, too, were often brought into native nations in this same way.

There is very little written testimony that remains telling us what Native Americans thought about the arrival of the Europeans. Accounts written by the first European settlers and traders describe the original inhabitants of North America as savages. We seldom hear what the Native Americans thought of the newcomers. Kondiaronk, a Huron chief, made the following observation in the 1600s to Baron De Lahontan, Lord Lieutenant of the French Colony in Newfoundland:

> *In earnest, my dear Brother, I am sorry for you from the bottom of my soul. Take my advice, and turn Huron; for I see plainly a vast difference between your condition and mine. I am master of my condition and mine. I am master of my own body, I have the absolute disposal of my self, I do what I please, I am the first and the last of my nation, I fear no man, and I depend only on the Great Spirit. Is it true or not?*   KONDIARONK *(Huron),* circa 1670

There was a stark physical contrast between Europeans and Native Americans. Many of the Europeans who arrived on the shores of North America were malnourished and weak after their long voyage. In many parts of North America, the average height of the Native Americans was greater than that of the average European. Both historians and archaeologists agree that around the fifteenth century, the average life expectancy of a European was somewhat less than that of a Native American. The varied diet of the Indians of the northeast coast was balanced and rich, and they were used to a hearty and active lifestyle. American Indian people bathed every day and took frequent steam baths in their sweat lodges. Until the mid-nineteenth century, western Europeans were deeply averse to bathing of any kind. Bathing was regarded as unhygienic and even sinful by Catholics and Protestants. In the words of historian Siegfried Giedion, prior to the mid-nineteenth century in western Europe, "There is no doubt that the most elementary sense of cleanliness was lacking."

In 1676, an unnamed chief of the Micmac people in Nova Scotia made these remarks to a group of Frenchmen who were trying to persuade the Micmac to build French-style houses and live in the French way.

> But why now do men of five to six feet in height need houses that are sixty to eighty? For in fact, as you know very well yourself, Patriarch—do we not find in our own all the conveniences and the advantages that you have with yours, such as reposing, drinking, sleeping, eating, and amusing ourselves with our friends when we wish? This is not all, my brother. Have you as much ingenuity and cleverness as the Indians, who carry their houses and their wigwams with them so that they may live wherever they

please? You are not as bold nor as stout as we, because when you go on a voyage you cannot carry upon your shoulders your home and your buildings....

And if we have not any longer among us any of those old men of a hundred and thirty to forty years, it is only because we are gradually adopting your manner of living, for experience is making it very plain that those of us who live longest are those who, despising your bread, your wine, and your brandy, are content with their natural food of beaver, of moose, of waterfowl and fish, in accord with the custom of our ancestors and of all the Micmac nation. Learn now, my brother once for all, because I must open to you my heart, there is no Indian who does not consider himself infinitely more happy and more powerful than the French.   MICMAC CHIEF, 1676

Many Europeans came to think that the Native American way of life had much to offer beyond their accustomed way of living. In 1750, a European named Peter Kalm kept a journal of his travels in North America, and observed how readily European settlers adopted an Indian lifestyle.

Some European men and women had a very hard lot in America as slaves sold into servitude for a specified number of years. Such indentured servants frequently ran away. Other European men and women were captured by Native Americans in battles or raids on European settlements. Often, such fugitive slaves and captives were adopted and made full members of Native American communities. Some adopted whites—such as Mary Jemison of the Seneca, or Blue Jacket, who became a chief of the Shawnee—became important people in their new native nations. Some even lived out their lives as Indians, refusing to return to their former lives as Europeans.

Many runaway African slaves or free African Americans also joined Indian communities contentedly, and became Indians. The Shinnecock of Long Island and the Wampanoag of Massachusetts have ancestors who were African American. Maroon communities of runaway slaves and Native Americans were found throughout the South, in the mountains and the deep swamps. Osceola, the famed Florida Seminole chief, was the child of a runaway slave and an Indian. Even those Native Americans who later came to have African slaves themselves, such as the Cherokee of the South, treated their slaves as near equals. Freed slaves often married American Indians. In fact, so many people of African descent intermarried with Native Americans, that a great many African Americans in the United States today are also of American Indian ancestry.

Frederick Jackson Turner was a historian of the early twentieth century whose writings on the American frontier, called the Turner Thesis, were very influential. Turner noted that only by living like Indians could colonists survive on the frontier. However, Turner's belief was that the Indians and the wilderness both had to be conquered and would disappear when real civilization arrived.

When they first came
we liked the whites

When they first came
we gave them food

When they first came
we liked the whites

CHEYENNE GHOST DANCE SONG, circa 1890

The attitude of these words from a Cheyenne song was common throughout America in the period of first contact. The Indians thought the Europeans to be strange, but interesting. Some, like the Cheyenne, at first described the whites as beautiful. Those first Europeans brought many useful things with them. Their jewelry, their clothing, their sharp knives and axes, their cooking utensils, their new powerful weapons, and even their ability to save their spoken words by making marks on paper, were admired by many Indians. Soon enough, the native people would see that the whites were also threatening and dangerous. So it was, as Lance Henson, a contemporary Cheyenne, explained to me, that the name for Europeans was chosen by the Cheyenne.

"We called them *veho*," he said. "That is the name for the trickster in our stories. Veho is the black widow spider. It is attractive, but deadly."

My own Abenaki people were among the first to encounter the European settlers, in the sixteenth century. At first there were only a few of them, and then there was a great flood of these strange new people. Our word for them, *awani-geek-nee-geek,* reflects our surprise. It means "Who are these people?" In 1618, English sea captains raided Wampanoag and Massachussett villages for Indian slaves. The arrival of the European slave ships also introduced diseases for which my people had no natural resistance. Between 1618 and 1619, epidemics of measles, smallpox, bubonic plague, cholera, tuberculosis, and yellow fever swept through Abenaki villages like fires that no water could quench. Thousands of people died, leaving virtually empty a coast that had once been heavily populated. In 1620, English settlers arrived on that same coast to establish the Plimoth Colony. Our people watched them at a distance, wary of being taken captive or infected with yet another fatal disease.

The first Native American to walk into Plimoth Plantation in 1620—at a time when the Pilgrims were in danger of starving—was an Abenaki named Samoset who had learned to speak a bit of English. "Welcome, English!" he said to them. A few days later, he returned with another man, a Pawtuxet Indian friend of his named Tisquantum. Tisquantum, or Squanto, as he came to be known, spoke fluent English because he had been taken to Europe as a slave. He had made his way back to the New England coast after many years in England.

Squanto's village had been on the site of Plimoth Plantation. But his people had sickened and died from a disease—perhaps smallpox or measles—brought among them by the European slave traders. His village was gone. Despite his years as a slave and his personal sorrows, Tisquantum decided to help the Europeans. He taught them how to grow native plants and showed them how to survive in the new land. Like so many other Native Americans, Squanto greeted the Europeans as friends and helped them. Without him, the first English colony in New England would not have survived.

European men, with their beards and mustaches, looked strange to the first Indians who saw them. They were so hairy, some of the people of the Great Plains refer to white men as "the northern bear" in their songs. In the Pacific Northwest, the Lutshootseed name for European literally translates as "upside-down face." Many white men were bald but had beards. Thus they looked as if their faces were upside down. In 1854, Maungwaduaus, an Ojibway, was brought to France with a group of other Indians to entertain the kings of France and Belgium, Napoléon III and Leopold I. He wrote this observation:

> *The French people wear much hair about their mouth, which makes them look bold and noble; but our friend Sasagon, who has no taste for beauty, says that it would puzzle any one of our people to find where the Frenchman's mouth is; and that a person having much hair round his mouth makes them look like one of our Indian dogs in North America when running away with a black squirrel in his mouth.* MAUNGWADUAUS *(Ojibway)*, 1854

> *Now this day*
> *My sun father,*
> *Now that you have come out standing*
>   *to your sacred place*
> *That from which we draw*
>   *the water of life,*
> *Prayer meal here I give to you,*
> *Your long life,*
> *Your old age,*
> *Your seeds,*
> *Your riches,*

Your power,

Your strong spirit,

All these to me may you grant.

ZUNI SUNRISE PRAYER

The Europeans also brought a new concept with them: time. My Abenaki people had no name for watch or clock. Our only measurements of time were through the changing of the seasons and the movements of the powerful, life-giving sun, the moon, and the stars. When the Europeans brought many clocks, my Abenaki ancestors saw that these things were important to Europeans. They needed a name in our language. So my ancestors carefully observed how clocks were used. The name they decided upon is still used to refer to watches or clocks today. *Papeezokwazik.* It means "that thing which makes much noise and does nothing useful."

It would be a long time before native people would be able to understand why clocks held such importance to non-native people. Carl Sweezy, an Arapaho Indian who was born in 1881, had this to say about the European idea of time:

Every white man seemed to have a great concern about time. We had our own names for the seasons and for the months that made up the year, but they were not the same as those the white man used. . . . It was a long time before we knew what the figures on the face of a clock meant, or why people looked at them before they ate their meals or started off to church. We had to learn that clocks have something to do with the hours and minutes that the white people mentioned so often. Hours, minutes, and seconds were such small divisions of time that we never thought of them. When the sun rose, when it was high in the sky, and when it set were all the divisions of the day that we ever found necessary when we followed the old Arapaho road. When we went on a hunting trip or to a sun dance, we counted time by sleeps.

White people, who did not try so hard to understand the ways of the Cheyenne and the Arapaho as we did to understand their ways, thought we were all lazy. That was because we took a different attitude toward time than theirs. We enjoyed time, they measured it.

CARL SWEEZY (*Arapaho*), 1966

Despite the cultural differences, contact between Indians and Europeans most often began in friendship and sharing. It is generally believed that the very first European to reach the western hemisphere was Cristóbal Colón [Columbus]. His journals of that first voyage contain much praise of the Taino people of the Caribbean for their generosity, their gentle friendship, and their open hearts. Yet that friendship and sharing did not continue. In the Caribbean, the Taino people soon became slaves, forced to work in the gold mines of Hispaniola.

The balance of power quickly shifted from the Native American to the European newcomer. In many places, the Indians tried to rely on diplomacy to avoid conflict with their new, more powerful neighbors. Few Indian nations were as skilled in diplomacy as the Iroquois, who were adept at making alliances, reminding the whites of the threat the Iroquois could pose as enemies, alternately asking for help and offering assistance, and always using their incredible power as orators.

For more than two centuries, the Iroquois were able to hold the balance of power between French and English by maintaining control of the Mohawk Valley, the gateway to the West and the fur trade. In 1684, the governors of New York and Virginia met in council with chiefs of the Onondaga, Cayuga, and Seneca, three of the five Iroquois nations. These words were said to the English governors by an unidentified Iroquois speaker:

> *Your Sachem is a great Sachem, and We are but a small People. But when the English first came to Manhatan, [to] Aragiske, and to Yakokranagary, they were then but a Small People, and we were Great. Then, because we found you a good People, we treated you civilly, and gave you Land. We hope therefore, now that you are Great and we Small, you will protect us from the French. If you do not, we shall loose all our Hunting and our Beaver. The French will get all the Beaver. They are now angry with us, because we carry our Beaver to our Brethren. . . .*
>
> *Our Fire burns in your Houses, and your Fire burns with us. We desire it be so always. But we will not [allow] that any of the great Penn's people settle upon the Susquehana River, for we have no other Land to leave to our Children. Our young People are Soldiers, and when they are disobliged they are like Wolves in the Woods, as you Sachem of Virginia very well know.*

ANONYMOUS *(Iroquois)*, 1684

The original generosity of the Indians was forgotten as the new settlers laid claim to more and more Indian land. The generation of giving would be followed by one of taking. Indian diplomacy could not hold back the tide of settlers. Yet, even though many Europeans seemed to forget that initial generosity, the Native Americans remembered how it all began. That first contact was often described in the speeches made to the following generations of newcomers.

One of the most eloquent of such speeches was given in 1792 by Red Jacket, a Seneca leader described as the greatest public speaker of his time. It is said that he trained his throat when he was a boy by standing at the edge of Niagara Falls and speaking, so that his voice became as deep and as strong as the powerful waters rushing over the falls. Red Jacket's words are an accurate description, from the Indian point of view, of what happened between that first generation, in which the newcomers were welcomed, and the second generation, in which the whites began to take by force what they had first been offered in friendship.

Brother! Listen to what we say. There was a time when our forefathers owned this great island. Their seats extended from the rising to the setting of the sun. The Great Spirit made it for the use of Indians. He had created the buffalo, the deer, and other animals for food. He made the bear and the deer, and their skins served us for food. He had scattered them over the country, and had taught us how to take them. He had caused the earth to produce corn for bread. All this he had done for his red children because he loved them. If we had any disputes about hunting grounds, they were generally settled without the shedding of much blood. But an evil day came upon us. Your forefathers crossed the great waters and landed upon this island. Their numbers were small. They found friends and not enemies. They told us they had fled from their own country for fear of wicked men, and had come here to enjoy their religion. They asked for a small seat. We took pity on them, granted their request and they sat down amongst us. We gave them corn and meat. They gave us poison in return. The white people had now found our country. Tidings were carried back and more came amongst us. Yet we did not fear them. We took them to be friends. They called us brothers. We believed them and gave them a large seat. At length their numbers had greatly increased. They wanted more land. They wanted our country.

RED JACKET/SAGOYEWATHA (*Seneca*), 1792

Nassauga
Root River
North People
Mississauga

Nikikos

Odawa

Niplssing
People of
the Lake
Nipissing

Atchirigough
People of the
Nose Pendant

Kinouri
Pike People

Atchougue

Quasonnin
Catfish

ALGONKIAN

Georgian
Bay

LAKE HURON
Michegame
The Big Lake

Odawa

Wendat
Huron

Huron
Hunting

Tionnontate
People of the Hills
Petun

Meskwahkihaki
Red Earths
Fox

LAKE ONTARIO
Ontario
Beautiful Water

Oneyoteaka
People of the
Standing Stone
Oneida

FIRE
NATIONS

Aandironon
Oueroukwaehronon
Swamp People

Atirouenigaga
Neutral
Antouaronons

Kayohkhono
People of the
Portage
Cayuga

Kahyeke
People
the Flint
Mohawk

Neutral Hunting Territory

Onontakeka
People of
the Village
on the Hill
Onondaga

People of the
Small Praries
Mascouten

INDIAN TERRITORY

Erie
Racoon Nation

IROQUOIS
Houdenosaunee
People of the Longhouse

Kiiaapoa
Kickapoo

LAKE ERIE

Wahbeshkegnokechegame
The White Water Lake

Riquehronon

Seneca

2. WHO OWNS THIS LAND?

I stood here, I stood there,

The clouds are speaking.

I say "You are the ruling power,

I do not understand, I only know what I am told,

You are the ruling power, you are now speaking.

The power is yours, O heavens."

PAWNEE SONG TO THE SKY

"Chenock eiuse wetompatimucks?" said Miantonomi of the Narragansett in 1637. "Did ever friends deal so with friends?" The Narragansett had allied themselves with the English in the war against the Pequot, but then were treated as enemies by the English. Similar words would be spoken frequently in the years following the time of welcoming, a time that did not last long. Although it dawned at different times—in the 1600s in New England, in the 1700s in the Southeast, in the 1800s in the plains and the far West—the day came all too quickly

when the newcomers wanted to do more than share the land. The newcomers wanted to own it all. This was a strange concept for native people, who saw the land as a sacred trust given to the people by the creator, not as something to be bought and sold. The earth did not belong to one people or one generation. It was meant to be taken care of for the generations to come.

The first permanent English settlement in North America was Jamestown in Virginia. There, the colonists were helped to establish their new community by the Powhatan Confederacy, an organization of thirty sovereign tribes including the Pamunkey, the Powhatan, and Mattaponi. In that same year, the Powhatan Confederacy of Nations entered into a treaty with the British colony of Virginia, providing for friendship and peace. Wahunsenacawh, the "Powhatan" or leader of the Powhatan Confederacy (most often recognized by contemporary people as the father of Pocahontas and most frequently called Powhatan), struggled until his death to maintain that peace with the English. Although the Indians provided them with corn to eat and taught them how to grow the tobacco that would eventually be the backbone of the colony's economy, history shows that the English did not treat them fairly.

The actions of Captain John Smith, the military leader of the colony, are one example. When the Virginia colony was low on corn, he simply gathered a group of armed men and forcibly took corn from the storehouses of the Indians, even though the Indians would probably have given the corn freely if they had been asked. It was such an incident in 1609 that inspired the following speech.

Why should you take by force that which you can have from us by love? Why should you destroy us who supply you with food? What can you get by war? We can hide our provisions and run into the woods; then you will starve for wronging your friends. You see us unarmed, and willing to supply your wants, if you come in a friendly manner and not with swords and guns, as to invade an enemy. I am not so simple as not to know it is better to eat good meat, lie well, and sleep quietly with my women and children, to laugh and be merry with the English....

WAHUNSENACAWH *(Powhatan)*, 1609

The five Iroquois tribes, centered in the area now known as New York State, had developed a unified league of nations by the coming of the Europeans. Their fifty chiefs, each chosen by the women of their clans, met in council to speak for their people in much the same way that present-day senators represent their constituents. The Iroquois described their confederacy as "The League of Peace," sheltered by the branches of a great tree under whose four white roots the war club was buried.

Because of their strategic location, their unity, and their skills in both diplomacy and war, the Iroquois were a pivotal force in the struggles that took place between the French and the English over the control of the American continent. In those "French and Indian Wars," the Iroquois usually allied themselves with the British. Yet, before the expulsion of the French from the area that would become the United States, the Iroquois made it plain that they preferred peace to war.

They saw themselves as free and independent people. No one—European or other—had the right to rule them.

One of the most eloquent statements of the Iroquois desire for peace and their passion for independence was made by the Onondaga chief Otreouti while acting as an ambassador to the French during peace negotiations with them in September 1664. (Otreouti was also known to the French as Garangula or La Grande Gueule, which means "big mouth," a name given because of his powerful oratory.) As they stood on the shores of Lake Ontario, the French governor held the calumet, the symbolic pipe of peace. The Iroquois title for the French governor was always "Yonnondio," just as the English governor was called "Corlaer." Despite the pipe of peace in his hands, that particular French governor began by threatening the Iroquois. It was an empty threat. The French weren't really prepared to attack the great stockaded villages or "castles," of the Iroquois. Not only was the Yonnondio outnumbered and far from Quebec, many of the men in his company of soldiers were ill with the fever. Otreouti listened patiently, a wampum belt whose designs symbolized this council in his hands, and made this response:

> Yonnondio! I honor you, and the warriors who are with me all likewise honor you. Your interpreter has finished your speech; I now begin mine. My words make haste to reach your ears. Listen to them. . . .
>
> Hear, Yonnondio! Take care for the future that so great a number of soldiers as appear there, do not choke the tree of peace planted in so small a fort. It will be a great loss if, after it had so easily taken root, you should stop its

growth and prevent it covering your country and ours with
its branches. I assure you, in the name of the Five Nations,
that our warriors shall dance to the calumet of peace under
its leaves. They shall remain quiet on their mats, and shall
never dig up the hatchet, till their brother Yonnondio, or
Corlaer, shall either jointly or separately endeavor to attack
the country, which the Great Spirit has given to our an-
cestors.   OTREOUTI *(Iroquois)*, 1664

European and American Indian cultures saw the land in very different ways. The English and the French, the Dutch and the Spanish and the Portugese all believed that land was something that could be purchased and owned. Once you held land, you could keep everyone else off it and do with it as you wished. It was a commodity to be bought and sold. Many of the so-called "land sales" made by Indians to whites were not viewed by the native people themselves as irrevocable, but merely as short-term leases or agreements allowing the whites to use that land in common with Indians. In the European view, the Indians had given up all claim to that land forever.

Yet that land had given birth to the people. For many native people the land, the very earth itself, was "Mother." How could anyone sell their mother? Corn could be eaten, but land would always remain. Even after selling land to white colonists, most Native Americans assumed they would still have the right to visit that land, to walk on it, to camp on it, to hunt and fish there.

The Iroquois thanksgiving address, given by a Faith Keeper at the start of every important meeting, describes the earth as

Mother. The Iroquois people say, in fact, that the oldest human ceremony is that of giving thanks to the earth, the mother of us all.

We return thanks to our mother, the earth, which sustains us. We thank thee, that thou hast caused her to yield so plentifully of her fruits. Cause that, in the season coming, she may not withhold of her fullness and leave any to suffer for want.

We return thanks to the rivers and streams, which run their courses upon the bosom of our mother, the earth. We thank thee, that thou hast supplied them with life, for our comfort and support. Grant that this blessing may continue.

We return thanks to all the herbs and plants of the earth. We thank thee, that in thy goodness thou hast blest them all, and given them strength to preserve our bodies healthy, and to cure us of the diseases inflicted upon us. . . .

We return thanks to the Three Sisters [corn, beans, and squash]. We thank thee, that thou hast provided them as the main supporters of our lives. We thank thee for the abundant harvest gathered in during the past season. We ask that our supporters may never fail us, and cause our children to suffer from want.   TRADITIONAL *(Iroquois)*

Smohalla, a holy man of the Wanapam people of the Pacific Northwest, expressed that same understanding of the earth as Mother.

You ask me to dig for stone. Shall I dig under her skin for bones? Then when I die I cannot enter her body to be born again.

You ask me to cut grass and make hay and sell it, and be rich like white men. But how dare I cut off my mother's hair?   SMOHALLA (*Wanapam*), 1850s

One of the most famous transfers of land in the New World was the "sale" of Manhattan.

In 1626, Peter Minuit made the "purchase" of Manhattan for sixty guilders worth of trade goods. [We don't know what those goods were.] The idea of buying the land was understood in two different ways by the people involved.

To the Europeans, ownership of land was synonymous with wealth, power, and prestige. To purchase land meant the exclusive right to live on and use the land.

To the Native people, the land belonged to everybody. It could not be bought or sold any more than water, air, or sunlight.

The Native people interpreted the trade goods as a gift from the Europeans to show their appreciation for the right to share the land.

They did not realize the Europeans meant to hold the land for their own exclusive use. Later, the Europeans put up a wall [hence the name Wall Street] to keep the Indians out.

GEORGETTA STONEFISH RYAN,
National Museum of the American Indian, 1992

Time and again, Indians spoke out when they were told they must accept white claims to the land and see the earth as nothing more than property to be bought and sold. Although the voices would be different over the next two centuries, the sentiments would be much the same. The earth, their mother, gave them life and would always provide for them as long as they remained true to her. Their love for their mother was unchanging and they would protect her with their lives.

Brothers, we must be one as the English are, or we shall soon all be destroyed. You know our fathers had plenty of deer and skins, and our plains were full of deer and turkeys. But, brothers, since these English have seized upon our country, they cut down the grass with scythes, and the trees with axes. Their cows and horses eat up the grass, and their hogs spoil our beds of clams; and finally, we shall starve to death! MIANTONOMI (*Narragansett*), 1642

What is one hundred years in comparison of the length of time since our claim began? since we came out of this ground? For we must tell you, that long before one hundred years, our ancestors came out of this very ground, and their children have remained here ever since.
CANASSATEGO (*Seneca*), 1744

Englishman!—Although you have conquered the French, you have not yet conquered us. We are not your slaves. These lakes, these woods and mountains, were left to us by our ancestors. They are our inheritance, and we will part with them to none. MINAVAVANA (*Chippewa*), 1761

Soon Indians realized how different the European ideas of land and ownership were from their own. Among many of the Native American tribes, signing documents agreeing to the sale of their land became an offense punishable by death. Yet there were many ways to convince Indian people to sign land-transfer documents. President Jefferson advocated the use of factory stores, where Indians would be given as much credit as they wanted to buy European-style goods. The usual result was that the Indians would incur so much debt that they were unable to pay when their bills came due. Then their land could be taken from them "legally" to pay off their debts.

Alcoholic beverages were unknown to most Native Americans before the coming of the Europeans. Since they had no previous knowledge of alcohol, Indians were not prepared. Often traders would first give away liberal quantities of rum in hopes that an Indian would be put at a disadvantage in bargaining after drinking. Benjamin Franklin, somewhat ironically, said that rum was a better weapon than guns, for if the Indians were given enough to drink they would kill one another. By the time of the next generation, alcoholism was a major problem among Native Americans.

See them coming into our towns with their rum! See them offering it to us with persuasive kindness. Hear them cry, "Drink! Drink!" and when we have drunk, and act like the crazed, behold these good whites, these men of a benevolent race, standing by, laughing among themselves, and saying, "Oh, what fools! What great fools the Shawanese are!" But who made them fools? Who are the cause of their madness?...

The whites tell us of their enlightened understanding, and the wisdom they have from Heaven, at the same time, they cheat us to their hearts' content. For we are as fools in their eyes, and they say among themselves, the Indians know nothing! The Indians understand nothing!

CHIEF GIESCHENATSI/HARD MAN (*Shawnee*), 1773

During this same period, in many ways, the English and French colonists were being greatly influenced by the Indians. They often joined the Indians, lived and dressed as they did, and became Indian. This sometimes caused problems for the Native Americans. As mentioned earlier, when whites came voluntarily or were taken captive, they were frequently adopted into Native American families. After a few seasons of living as Indians, many of those former captives devoted themselves wholeheartedly to their new culture. Yet agreements between whites and Indians usually made the return of white captives part of the deal. As Chief Gieschenatsi explained to the Continental Congress in 1776, these white captives often would resist repatriation, refusing to return to the white settlements and hiding in the woods until the threat of being parted from their new families was gone. Their skins were still white, but their hearts were red.

Brothers of Virginia, You have told us to send all your Flesh & Blood—all that we could find we have sent to you, but some have run away, & others we have since collected. We will deliver them all up, when they are called for. You told us last fall to expect to see you at Pittsburgh this Spring, where you would finish an everlasting Peace with us. This we still look for, & wait to hear from you.

CHIEF GIESCHENATSI/HARD MAN *(Shawnee)*, 1776

Despite the sympathy that many white Americans felt for the Indian, the dispossession continued. By the early nineteenth century, the tribes of the Midwest and the South were feeling this pressure. Although they had given the newcomers a place to stay and often welcomed them as guests, the Indians were now being treated as foreigners to be expelled from their own native lands.

Brothers, I have listened to many talks from our great father. When he first came over the wide waters, he was but a little man, very little. His legs were cramped by sitting long in his big boat, and he begged for a little land to light his fire on. But when the white man had warmed himself before the Indians' fire and filled himself with their hominy, he became very large. With a step he bestrode the mountains, and his feet covered the plains and the valleys. His hand grasped the eastern and western sea, and his head rested on the moon. Then he became our Great Father. He loved his red children, and he said, "Get a little further, lest I tread on thee."

Brothers! I have listened to a great many talks from our great father. But they always began and ended in this— "Get a little further; you are too near me."

SPECKLED SNAKE *(Creek)*, 1829

*The Great Spirit created this country for the use and bene-
fit of his red children and placed them in full possession
of it, and we were happy and contented. Why did he send
the palefaces across the great ocean to take it from us?
When they landed on our territory they were received
as long-absent brothers whom the Great Spirit had returned to us. Food and rest were freely given them by our
fathers, who treated them all the more kindly on account
of their weak and helpless condition. Had our fathers
the desire, they could have crushed the intruders out of
existence with the same ease we kill the blood-sucking
mosquitoes.*

BLACK HAWK/MAKATAIMESHEKIAKIAK *(Mesquakie)*, 1832

By the middle of the nineteenth century, the conflict over
the land and its ownership shifted west. The Louisiana Purchase, the War with Mexico, and the Gadsden Purchase had
given the United States "legal" title from the great Mississippi
River to the Pacific Ocean. Yet all of those legal titles, whether
gained by purchase or by war, had been given to the United
States by other European nations. To the Native American
nations within that great expanse of land, those European titles
to the land meant nothing.

For the native peoples of the West, the issue was not only
the land, but also the great herds of buffalo that sustained
every aspect of their lives. The buffalo provided them with
food and clothing. The skins covered their lodges, the bones
made tools, and it was the center of many of their most important religious ceremonies. The protection of the buffalo
from slaughter was a major concern for such nations as the

Cheyenne and Comanche, the Lakota and the Kiowa, and they expressed that concern.

> *I love the land and the buffalo and will not part with it. I want you to understand well what I say....*
>
> *A long time ago this land belonged to our fathers; but when I go up to the river I see camps of soldiers on its banks. These soldiers cut down my timber; they kill my buffalo; and when I see that, my heart feels like bursting; I feel sorry. I have spoken.*   SATANTA *(Kiowa)*, 1867

To be able to hunt the buffalo was the center of life. If that center was threatened, they could die. Such leaders as Ten Bears would speak words of warning.

> *My heart is filled with joy when I see you here, as the brooks fill with water when the snow melts in the spring; and I feel glad as the ponies do when the fresh grass starts in the beginning of the year....*
>
> *My people have never first drawn a bow or fired a gun against the whites. There has been trouble on the line between us, and my young men have danced the war-dance. But it was not begun by us. It was you who sent the first soldier and we who sent out the second. Two years ago I came upon this road, following the buffalo...but the soldiers fired on us, and since that time there has been a noise like that of a thunderstorm, and we have not known which way to go....*
>
> *But there are things which you have said to me which I do not like. They were not sweet like sugar, but bitter*

like gourds. You said that you wanted to put us upon a reservation, to build our houses and make us medicine lodges. I do not want them. I was born upon the prairie, where the wind blew free, and there was nothing to break the light of the sun.

I was born where there were no enclosures, and where everything drew a free breath. I want to die there, and not within walls. I know every stream and every wood between the Rio Grande and the Arkansas. I have hunted and lived over that country. I lived like my fathers before me, and like them, I lived happily. . . .

The white man has the country which we loved and we only wish to wander on the prairie until we die. Any good thing you say to me shall not be forgotten. I shall carry it as near to my heart as my children, and it shall be as often on my tongue as the name of the Great Spirit. I want no blood upon my land to stain the grass. I want it all clear and pure, and I wish it so, that all who go through among my people may find peace when they come in and leave it when they go out.

TEN BEARS (*Comanche*), 1867

At last, after trying every other way to coexist, it seemed for Native Americans that there was no other way but to resist. In a newspaper interview in 1879, Sitting Bull, the great Lakota leader, made this simple statement, a prophecy of the harder times to come.

I will remain what I am until I die, a hunter, and when there are no buffalo or other game I will send my children

to hunt and live on prairie mice, for where an Indian is
shut up in one place his body becomes weak.

SITTING BULL/TATANKA IYOTAKE *(Hunkpapa Lakota)*, 1879

And what, Sitting Bull was asked, about the American soldiers, the Long Knives, who were trying to force the Lakotas onto reservations?

We will avoid them if we can. If we cannot, we will fight.

SITTING BULL/TATANKA IYOTAKE *(Hunkpapa Lakota)*, 1879

The life my people want is a life of freedom.

SITTING BULL (Hunkpapa Lakota)

3. RESISTANCE

Now! Blue Thunder, very quickly

You have just come to make a home.

Now! You have come to join the body.

Now! Red Thunder!

CHEROKEE CHARM FOR
PROTECTION AND SUCCESS
IN BATTLE

AS TIME WENT ON and the threats to their lands grew, more and more native leaders came to the conclusion that accommodation and cooperation were no longer possible. Even the lands promised to them in solemn councils and treaty agreements were being invaded. Soon there would be no room for the Indians. They decided to resist.

One of the early wars of resistance was led by Manitonquat in 1675. When the whites violated their treaty with the

Indians, Manitonquat, who was known to the colonists as King Philip, led a confederacy against the towns of New England. William Apess, a Pequot who became a Methodist minister, gave a eulogy for King Philip in Boston in 1836. Apess, who was then thirty-eight years old, vanished soon after that sermon, never to be seen again. No one knows how or when he died, although many believe they know why.

> It does appear that every Indian heart had been lighted at the council fires at Philip's speech, and that the forest was literally alive with this injured race. And now town after town fell before them. The Pilgrims with their forces were ever marching in one direction, while Philip and his forces were marching in another, burning all before them, until Middleborough, Taunton, and Dartmouth were laid in ruins and forsaken by its inhabitants. . . .
>
> This was a sorry time to them; the Pilgrims, however, reinforced, but ordered a retreat, supposing it impossible for Philip to escape, and knowing his forces to be great, it was conjectured by some to build a fort to starve him out, as he had lost but few men in the fight. The situation of Philip was rather peculiar, as there was but one outlet to the swamp, and the river before him nearly seven miles to descend. The Pilgrims placed a guard around the swamp for 13 days, which gave Philip and his men time to prepare canoes to make good his retreat; in which he did, to the Connecticut river, and in his retreat lost but fourteen men. We may look upon this move of Philip's to be equal, if not superior to that of Washington crossing the Delaware.
>
> WILLIAM APESS (*Pequot*), 1836

The warfare that ensued between the native people and the newcomers—first Dutch, Spanish, French, and British, and then the new American nation—was a strange new kind of warfare for many of the native leaders.

> *Instead of stealing upon each other and taking every advantage to kill the enemy and save their own people, as we do (which, with us, is considered good policy in a war chief), they march out, in open daylight, and fight, regardless of the number of warriors they may lose! After the battle is over, they retire to feast, and drink wine, as if nothing had happened; after which, they make a statement in writing, of what they have done—each party claiming the victory! and neither giving an account of half the number that have been killed on their own side. They all fought like braves, but would not do to lead a war party with us. Our maxim is "to kill the enemy and save our own men." Those chiefs would do to paddle a canoe, but not to steer it.*
>
> BLACK HAWK/MAKATAIMESHEKIAKIAK *(Mesquakie)*, 1834

From east coast to west coast, from north to south, the story was the same. The Indians fought with skill and bravery, but they were outnumbered, they were weakened by disease, and they were betrayed by their allies—both white and Indian. Had it not been for the decimation of Native Americans by wave after wave of lethal diseases from Europe, such as the smallpox that ravaged the Aztec, the European conquest of the New World might never have succeeded. There is evidence that in some times whites, such as Sir Jeffrey Amherst during the French and Indian Wars, exposed Indians to small-pox deliberately. It has been estimated that more than two thousand of Amherst's Indian enemies, the Ottawa and their allies, were struck down by smallpox in this way.

Could it not be contrived to send the Small Pox among those disaffected tribes of Indians?... You will do well to try to innoculate the Indians by means of blankets, as well as to try every other method that can serve to extirpate this execrable race. SIR JEFFREY AMHERST, 1763

The Ottawas were greatly reduced in numbers on account of the small-pox which they brought from Montreal during the French war with Great Britain. This small-pox was sold to them shut up in a tin box, with the strict injunction not to open their box on their way homeward, but only when they should reach their country; and that this box contained something that would do them great good, and their people.... Accordingly, after they reached home they opened the box; but behold there was another tin box inside, smaller. They took it out and opened the second box, and behold, still there was another box inside the second box, smaller yet. So they kept on this way till they came to a very small box, which was no more than an inch long; and when they opened the last one they found nothing but mouldy particles in the last box. They wondered very much what it was, and a great many closely inspected to try to find out what it meant. But alas, alas! pretty soon burst out a terrible sickness among them. The great Indian doctors themselves were taken sick and died. The tradition says it was indeed terrible and awful. Every one taken with it was sure to die. Lodge after lodge was totally vacated—nothing but the dead bodies lying here and there in their lodges—entire families swept off with the ravages of this terrible disease.

CHIEF ANDREW J. BLACKBIRD *(Chippewa)*, 1887

*Strike the earth
with your great curved horns
We will hear the sound
and our hearts will be strong
When we go to war
give us your strength
Strike the earth
with your great curved horns
Lead us forth to the fight.*

OJIBWAY SONG
TO THE BUFFALO

*O Wakonda, you see me a poor man
Have pity on me.
I got to war to revenge the death of my brother.
Let no enemies surprise me.
Give me the bows and arrows of my enemies.
Give me their guns.
Give me their horses.
I will remember.
Have pity on me.*

ASSINIBOINE WARRIOR'S PRAYER

It was also never so simple a thing as the Native American against the European. Different native nations formed alliances with one another and with the various European powers attempting to gain control of the continent. When the Dutch fought against the Mahican and Lenape peoples in the early seventeenth century, they did so with the help of allies from other Indian nations. In the early eighteenth century, the Abenaki were allies of the French, who fought against the British and their Iroquois allies. When the Creek fought against the United States in the early nineteenth century, the Cherokee fought against them as allies of the Americans. When Custer was defeated at Little Big Horn, he was guided by Crow Indian scouts.

These alliances occurred in part because some European leaders, such as Sir William Johnson in the early eighteenth century, treated their Indian allies with respect and fairness and were well liked in return. The name the Mohawk gave Johnson, Warrahiyehgey, "He Who Does Much Honest Business," is an indication of how they responded to him. The strong bond of friendship he formed was a major reason the Mohawk nation fought against the French and also chose to support the British side in the American Revolution.

Native American leaders also saw that they did not have the numbers or the weapons of war necessary to defend their people. Two of the greatest resistance leaders tried to save their people by making alliances with other native nations and with the European nation they thought was most sympathetic to the Indian. These men, whose names have become legend to white and Indian alike, were Pontiac and Tecumseh.

Born in 1720, near present-day Fort Wayne, Indiana,

Pontiac, an Ottawa Indian, was a charismatic leader. One of the most gifted speakers of his time, he possessed a powerful voice that matched the eloquence of his words. The historian Frances Parkman said of him, "The American forest never produced a man more shrewd, politic and ambitious." His visionary oratory brought together the widest alliance of Indian nations that had yet joined in a common cause. Between 1754 and 1760, the British and French fought what would be called the French and Indian Wars across the northeastern part of the North American continent. The British colonists and soldiers were pushing farther and farther west at the time of this alliance, while the French appeared not to have such territorial aims at the expense of the Indians. For this reason, Pontiac treated the French as his allies, the British as his enemies.

On April 27, before his attack on Detroit, he made the speech from which the following excerpt, rewritten in modern English, is taken. He tells the story of a vision experienced by a Delaware Indian prophet. It is an allegory whose substance would be repeated again and again in the visions of later Native American prophets: Only a return to the customs of their ancestors can save the people from destruction. The beautiful woman clothed in white, who is the Delaware's first helper, is symbolic of the guiding power of women within the native cultures of the Northeast, much like other powerful and benevolent female beings, such as the Corn Maiden, who brought the great gift of maize. Dependence upon European trade goods was already so great by Pontiac's time that most of the native people of the Great Lakes region had abandoned important crafts, such as pottery making. They could no longer survive without the trade goods of the whites.

A Delaware Indian wanted to learn wisdom from the Master of Life. Not knowing where to find him, he fasted and dreamed. So it was revealed to him, that, by moving forward in a straight, undeviating course, he would reach the place of the Great Spirit. On the evening of the eighth day, he stopped by the side of a brook at the edge of a meadow, where he saw three large openings in the woods before him, and three well-beaten paths which entered them. His wonder increased when, after it had grown dark, the three paths were more clearly visible than ever. Leaving his fire, he crossed the meadow, and entered the largest of the three openings. A bright flame sprang out of the ground before him. In great amazement, he turned back, and entered the second path. Again, the bright flame sprang from the ground. Determined to continue, he took the last of the three paths. On this he journeyed a whole day without interruption. At length, emerging from the forest, he saw before him a vast mountain, of dazzling whiteness. So steep was the ascent that the Indian thought it hopeless to go farther, and looked around him in despair. At that moment he saw, seated at some distance above, the figure of a beautiful woman in white, who arose as he looked upon her, and spoke to him.

"How can you hope, weighed down as you are, to succeed? Go down to the foot of the mountain, throw away your gun, your ammunition, your provisions and your clothing; wash yourself in the stream which flows there, and you will then be prepared to stand before the Master of Life."

The Indian obeyed, and again began to climb. After

great toil and suffering, he found himself at the summit.
A rich and beautiful plain spread before him, and at a
little distance he saw three great villages, far superior to
the small villages of the Delawares. As he approached the
largest, and stood hesitating whether he should enter, a
man gorgeously attired stepped forth and, taking him by
the hand, brought him into the presence of the Great
Spirit, where the Indian stood amazed at the indescribable
splendor which surrounded him. The Great Spirit told him
to sit, and spoke to him:

"I am the Maker of heaven and earth, the trees, lakes,
rivers, and all things else. I am the Maker of mankind;
and because I love you, you must do my will. The land on
which you live I have made for you, and not for others.
Why do you suffer the white men to dwell among you? My
children, you have forgotten the customs and traditions of
your forefathers. Why do you not clothe yourselves in skins,
as they did, and use the bows and arrows, and the stone-
pointed lances, which they used? You have bought guns,
knives, kettles, and blankets from the white men, until you
can no longer do without them; and, what is worse, you
have drunk the poison fire-water, which turns you into
fools. Fling all these things away; live as your wise fore-
fathers lived before you. And as for these English—these
dogs dressed in red who have come to rob you of your
hunting grounds, and drive away the game—you just lift
the hatchet against them. Wipe them from the face of the
earth, and then you will win my favor back again, and
once more be happy and prosperous. The children of your
great father, the King of France, are not like the English.

Never forget they are your brethren. They are very dear to me, for they love the red men, and understand the true mode of worshipping me." PONTIAC *(Ottawa)*, 1763

Although Pontiac had pledged his loyalty to them, when he was laying seige to the British Fort Detroit, the French never came to his aid and he was forced to lift the seige. In 1763, on May 23, he spoke these words to his European allies:

Recollect the war you had seventeen years ago, and the part I took in it. The Northern nations combined together, and came to destroy you. Who defended you? Was it not myself and my young men? The great chief, Mackinac, said in Council that he would carry to his native village the head of your chief warrior, and that he would eat his heart and drink his blood. Did I not then join you, and go to his camp and say to him, if he wished to kill the French he must first pass over my body and the bodies of my young men? Did I not take hold of the tomahawk with you, and aid you in fighting your battles with Mackinac, and driving him home to his country? Why do you think I would turn my arms against you? Am I not the same French Pontiac, who assisted you seventeen years ago?

PONTIAC *(Ottawa)*, 1763

Caught between warring groups of Europeans, first the English and the French, and then the English and the American colonists (the Long-Knives), many native leaders found themselves forced to fight and choose sides in battles that always seemed to end with the Indians as the eventual losers.

It is better for the red men to die like warriors than to diminish away by inches. Now is the time to begin. If we fight like men, we may hope to enlarge our bounds. The Cherokees have a hatchet that was brought to you six years ago. Your brothers the Shawnees hope you will take it up and use it immediately.   CORNSTALK *(Shawnee),* 1776

Father! Pay attention to what I am going to say. While you, Father, are setting me on your enemy, much in the same manner as a hunter sets his dog on the game; whilst I am in the act of rushing on that enemy of yours, with the bloody destructive weapon you gave me, I may, perchance, happen to look back to the place from whence you started me, and what shall I see? Perhaps I may see my father shaking hands with the Long-Knives; yes, with those very people he now calls his enemies. I may then see him laugh at my folly for having obeyed his orders; and yet I am risking my life at his command!—Father! keep what I have said in remembrance.

CAPTAIN PIPE/HOPOCAN *(Delaware),* 1781

Tecumseh (as his name was recorded by European Americans) was a Shawnee chief and one of the most charismatic native leaders ever to walk this continent. The idea of his name, not easily translated into English, is something like a combination of "Shooting Star" and "Panther Leaping Across the Sky." His dream was to ally all the native nations to hold back the onrush of white settlers across the Appalachians.

In 1810, he spoke of that dream in his speech to Governor William Henry Harrison, in which he contended that Indian land could not be sold to the whites because all Native Americans held it in common.

It is true I am a Shawnee. My forefathers were warriors. Their son is a warrior. From them I take my existence; and from my tribe I take nothing. I am the maker of my own fortune; and oh! that I could make that of my red people, and of my country, as great as the conceptions of my mind, when I think of the Spirit that rules the universe. I would not then come to Governor Harrison, to ask him to tear the treaty, and to obliterate the landmark; but I would say to him, Sir, you have liberty to return to your own country. The being within, communing with past ages, tells me, that once, nor until lately, there was no white man on this continent. That it then all belonged to red men, children of the same parents, placed on it by the Great Spirit that made them, to keep it, to traverse it, to enjoy its productions, and to fill it with the same race. Once, a happy race. Since made miserable by the white people, who are never contented, but always encroaching. The way, and the only way to check and stop this evil, is, for all the red men to unite in claiming a common and equal right in the land, as it was at first, and should be yet; for it was never divided, but belongs to all, for the use of each. That no part has a right to sell, even to each other, much less to strangers; those who want all, and will not do with less. The white people have no right to take the land from the Indians, because they had it first; it is theirs. They may sell, but all must join. Any sale not made by all is not valid. The late sale is bad. It was made by a part only. Part do not know how to sell. It requires all to make a bargain for all. All red men have equal rights to the unoccupied land. The right of occupancy is as good in one place as in another. There cannot be two occupants in the same place. The first excludes all others. It is not so in hunting or travelling; for there the same ground will serve many as they follow each other all day; but the camp is stationary and that is occupancy. It belongs to the first who sits down on his blanket or skins, which he has thrown on the ground, and till he leaves it no other has a right.

TECUMSEH *(Shawnee)*, 1810

Tecumseh's dream never became a reality. Peoples such as the Cherokee and Choctaw refused to join his cause, preferring to remain in friendship with the Americans.

In white society a government could command its men to fight in an army. In the often extreme democracy of an Indian society, a chief could attempt to convince the warriors to join his side, but he could never command them to do so. Chief Pushmataha's response to one of Tecumseh's speeches is typical of this idea. Further, though it isn't mentioned directly by Pushmataha, the decision to fight was never the men's alone. Among such nations as Pushmataha's Choctaw, the women had a large voice in deciding whether there would be war or peace.

Tecumseh's words to the wavering Choctaw were spoken with fiery eloquence. They reflect the history of his own

Shawnee people, who had been pushed farther and farther from their original homelands.

> *Let us form one body, one heart, and defend to the last warrior our country, our homes, our liberty, and the graves of our fathers.* TECUMSEH (*Shawnee*), 1811

Pushmataha was both a brave leader of his people and a pragmatist. The Choctaw had a long history of alliance with the whites, and it was Pushmataha's sincere belief that Tecumseh's way was wrong. The friendship between the Choctaw and their white neighbors was a very real one. When the removal of the Choctaw to Indian Territory took place, many of the white people of Mississippi condemned it. Others turned a blind eye to those few Choctaw who quietly remained in Mississippi or, in some cases, gave them help.

> *The white Americans buy our skins, our corn, our cotton, our surplus game, our baskets, and other wares, and they give us in fair exchange their cloth, their guns, their tools, implements, and other things which the Choctaw need but do not make. It is true we have befriended them, but who will deny that these acts of friendship have been abundantly reciprocated? They have given us cotton gins, which simplify the spinning and sale of our cotton; they have encouraged and helped us in the production of our crops; they have taken many of our wives into their homes to teach them useful things and pay them for their work while*

learning; they teach our children to read and write from their books. You all remember the dreadful epidemic visited upon us last winter. During its darkest hours these neighbors whom we are now urged to attack responded generously to our needs. They doctored our sick; they clothed our suffering; they fed our hungry....

PUSHMATAHA *(Choctaw)*, 1811

Seventeen years after the death of Tecumseh and six years after Pushmataha's death, with the Treaty of Dancing Rabbit Creek on September 27, 1830, the Choctaw would be the first nation to be removed west of the Mississippi to Indian Territory. As Tecumseh had prophesied, the majority of the Choctaw people would be forced to leave their homes in Mississippi, never to return, although his most dire prediction, the total extermination of the Indian, would not come to pass.

Tecumseh continued to ally himself with the British during the War of 1812 and held the rank of brigadier general. There, in 1813, five decades after the French had deserted the Indian—when they betrayed their ally Pontiac—the British would do much the same. In the midst of a battle, they would retreat from the field, leaving the Indians alone to face the American soldiers. Tecumseh's words of scorn spoken on September 18, 1813, are echoed by those of many before and after him who found that promises between Native Americans and Europeans were not often kept.

We are much astonished to see our father tying everything up and preparing to run away without letting his red children know what his intentions are. You always told us to remain here and take care of our lands; it made our hearts glad to hear that was your wish. You always told us you would never draw your foot off British ground; but now, Father, we see you are drawing back, and we are sorry our father is doing so without seeing the enemy. We must compare our father's conduct to a fat animal, that carries its tail upon its back, but when frightened it drops it between its legs and runs off.... TECUMSEH *(Shawnee),* 1813

Soldiers,
You fled.

Even the Eagle dies.
TETON SIOUX SONG

Let us all mount up our horses.
When I am old, I shall die.
I might die at any time.
I want to find out how it is.
It is like going up over a divide.
WANTS-TO-DIE *(Crow),*
date unknown

The first half of the nineteenth century saw the Indians being forced from the American South. By the mid-1800s, the conflict had shifted west. Although such native nations as the Sioux and Cheyenne would be portrayed as warlike, many of their most important leaders constantly spoke on behalf of peace. As it was among the native people east of the Mississippi, a good war leader was considered one who brought all of his warriors home alive from battle. When they did decide to take to the battlefield, they went in defense of their people and their lands. Despite the efforts of good-hearted people on all sides, a series of wars was fought between whites and one Native American nation after another, ending with the bloody massacre of Lakota people at Wounded Knee in 1890.

The Great Sioux Uprising of 1862 in Minnesota was caused by the failure of the United States to live up to its agreement with the Sioux—who had given up their lands and moved to a reservation because they had been promised such bare necessities as food and clothing. When corrupt traders, working hand in hand with corrupt government officials, pocketed the government payments instead of supplying provisions, the Indians complained. They were ignored.

Ten years before the uprising, which would bring the loss of many lives, white and Indian alike, the Dakota Sioux Chief Red Iron spoke to Governor Ramsey.

The snow is on the ground, and we have been waiting a long time to get our money. We are poor; you have plenty. Your fires are warm. Your teepees keep out the cold. We have been waiting a long time for our moneys. Our hunting-season is past. A great many of our people are sick, for being hungry. We may die because you will not pay us. We may die, but if we do we will leave our bones on the ground, that our Great Father may see where his Dakota

children died. We are very poor. We have sold our hunting
grounds and the graves of our fathers. We have sold our
own graves. We have no place to bury our dead. . . .

RED IRON (Sisseton Dakota), 1852

When the uprising finally came in 1862, it was reluctantly
led by Taoyateduta, Chief Little Crow, of the Santee Dakota.
Even as he entered the conflict, he knew it would be a losing
battle.

Taoyateduta is not a coward, and he is not a fool. . . . You
are like little children: you do not know what you are
doing. . . .

You are like dogs in the Hot Moon when they run mad
and snap at their own shadows. We are only little herds of
buffalo left scattered; the great herds are like the locusts
when they fly so thick that the whole sky is a snowstorm.
You may kill one—two—ten, as many as leaves in the
forest yonder, and their brothers will not miss them. Kill
one—two—ten, and ten times ten will come to kill you.
Count your fingers all day long and white men with guns
will come faster than you can count. . . .

You will die like the rabbits when the hungry wolves
hunt them in the Hard Moon.

Taoyateduta is not a coward: he will die with you.

LITTLE CROW/TAOYATEDUTA (Santee Dakota), 1862

The uprising ended in the Dakota's defeat. Two thousand
Dakota were imprisoned, and on November 5, 303 Dakota

men were sentenced to death. President Lincoln interceded, and in the end, 38 of them were hung. Over 1,300 Santee Dakota were shipped west to the barren Crow Creek reserve in Dakota Territory on the Missouri River, where almost a third died before the end of the winter.

It might be said that the turning point came soon after, with the buffalo wars. The Plains Indians saw that the end of the buffalo would be the end of their independent way of life. In 1874, the tribes of the southern plains rose up to try to drive out the buffalo hunters who were destroying the animals that sustained the lives of a dozen different tribes. The destruction of the buffalo, by the late 1800s, was not done by accident but by government policy. With the U.S. Army unable to defeat the southern plains tribes in open warfare, the destruction of the tribes' source of life was thought by many prominent military leaders to be the only solution.

[Buffalo hunters] have done more in the last two years to settle the vexed Indian question than the entire regular army has done in the past thirty years. They are destroying the Indians' commissary. . . . For the sake of lasting peace let them kill, skin, and sell until the buffaloes are exterminated. Then your prairies can be covered with speckled cattle and the festive cowboy. . . .

GENERAL PHILIP SHERIDAN, 1874

The Kiowa, Comanche, Cheyenne, and Arapaho, the tribes of the southern plains, offered peace and received deception in return. In October 1865, these four Indian nations agreed to the Little Arkansas Treaty, which said the tribes would be given a huge reservation in the area of the Texas Panhandle. Unfortunately for the Indians, that land existed only on paper. They found themselves homeless.

The white man grows jealous of his red brother. The white man once came to trade, now he comes as a soldier. He once put his trust in our friendship and wanted no shield but our fidelity. But now he builds forts and plants big guns on their walls. He once gave us arms and bade us hunt the game. He now covers his face with the cloud of jealousy and anger and tells us to be gone, as an offended master speaks to his dog.

SITTING BEAR/SATANK *(Kiowa),* 1867

By the 1870s, it was clear that the buffalo would soon be gone. The Cheyenne, Arapaho, Comanche, and Kiowa tried again and again to convince the government to protect the herds as the treaties had promised. But no heed was paid to their words. In 1874 they fought to try to save the last of the herds in a final act of desperation.

Your people make big talk and sometimes make war, if an Indian kills a white man's ox to keep his wife and family from starving; what do you think my people ought to say

when they see their buffalo killed by your race when you
are not hungry?   CHIEF LITTLE ROBE *(Cheyenne),* 1874

The buffalo is our money. It is our only resource to buy
what we need and do not receive from the government.
The robes we can prepare and trade. We love them just as
the white man loves his money. Just as it makes a white
man feel to have his money carried away, so it makes us
feel to see others killing and stealing our buffaloes, which
are our cattle given to us by the Great Father above to
provide us meat to eat and means to get things to wear.
[Tenses changed.]   STRIKING EAGLE *(Kiowa),* 1874

The final, most dramatic years of open warfare between
whites and Native Americans would be between 1860 and
1890. In these three decades, the names of the Native
American warriors and chiefs who resisted as best they
could—Red Cloud, Sitting Bull, and Crazy Horse of the Lakota Sioux, Cochise and Geronimo of the Apache, and Chief
Joseph of the Nez Perce—would become known throughout
the world, and they remain famous to this day. Yet these men
were reluctant to make war on whites; they sought only to
protect their people.

Sitting Bull typifies the image and the warrior spirit of the
Indian. His stance was almost always one of resistance. It
suited his name, Tatanka Iyotake, which implies the idea of
the bull buffalo that will not be moved when its mind is made
up. The Lakota people knew that the buffalo, unlike other

animals, always faced into the storm. That was Sitting Bull. When other Indians took the presents of the whites and moved in to live near the whites' forts, Sitting Bull headed out to the buffalo country.

Look at me. See if I am poor, or my people either. The whites may get me at last, as you say, but I will have good times till then. You are fools to make yourselves slaves to a piece of fat bacon, some hard-tack, and a little sugar and coffee.

SITTING BULL/TATANKA IYOTAKE *(Hunkpapa Lakota),* 1867

Even in 1883, after having been confined at Fort Randall, Sitting Bull would say:

White men like to dig in the ground for their food. My people prefer to hunt the buffalo as their fathers did. White men like to stay in one place. My people want to move their teepees here and there to the different hunting grounds. The life of white men is slavery. They are prisoners in towns or farms. The life my people want is a life of freedom. I have seen nothing that a white man has, houses or railways or clothing or food, that is as good as the right to move in the open country, and live in our own fashion.

SITTING BULL/TATANKA IYOTAKE *(Hunkpapa Lakota),* 1883

You, sun, my relative,
Be good going down at sunset.
We lay down to sleep,
We want to feel good.

Go on your course many times.
Make good things for the people.

Make me always as I am now.

HAVASUPAI PRAYER

I will fight no more forever.

CHIEF JOSEPH (Nez Perce)

4. THE BREAKING OF THE CIRCLE

Dry is my tongue from marching

Oh, my elder brother, Oh, my elder brother.

Dry is my tongue from marching,

And death draws near to me ...

OSAGE WAR SONG

FROM THE East Coast to the West Coast, one after another, the tribes that resisted were defeated. For many, like Black Elk, the Lakota medicine man, this seemed to be the end of their cultures, the breaking of the sacred hoop.

In speeches, in letters, and even in books, native leaders responded to their defeats and the destruction of their dreams of continued self-determination. The words of Chief Joseph of the Nez Perce—who had always been allies of the whites— are heartrending in their sorrow.

I am tired of fighting. Our chiefs are killed. Looking Glass is dead. Too-hool-hoot-suit is dead. The old men are all dead. It is the young men who say no and yes. He who led the young men is dead. It is cold and we have no blankets. The little children are freezing to death. My people, some of them, have run away to the hills and have no blankets, no food. No one knows where they are—perhaps they are freezing to death. I want to have time to look for my children and see how many of them I can find. Maybe I shall find them among the dead. Hear me, my chiefs, I am tired. My heart is sad and sick. From where the sun now stands I will fight no more forever.

CHIEF JOSEPH/IN-MUT-TOO-YAH-LAT-LAT (*Nez Perce*), 1877

During the Revolution, the Great League of the Iroquois had been divided in its loyalties. The league itself could come to no decision as to which side it would unanimously support. The council fire was symbolically covered and neutrality urged upon the six member nations of Mohawk, Oneida, Onondaga, Cayuga, Seneca, and Tuscarora (who had recently joined the league after being dispossessed of their lands in North Carolina and migrating north). In effect, each of the six nations could make up their own minds what they would do. Many Iroquois chose to support the British, particularly the Seneca and the Mohawk. The Oneida and Tuscarora, in large part, fought on the side of the American colonists.

After the war's end, a large party of those who supported the British, led by the Mohawk Joseph Brant, crossed into Canada and settled on lands deeded to them by the British crown, breaking the unity of the Six Nations of the Iroquois.

All the Iroquois who remained in what was now the United States—a nation led by George Washington, the man the Iroquois called "The Town Destroyer"—found themselves pushed into small enclaves and treated as defeated enemies after the war ended and the treaty of Fort Stanwyx was forced upon them.

> *When your army entered the country of the Six Nations, we called you the town destroyer; and to this day, when your name is heard, our women look behind them and turn pale, and our children cling close to the necks of their mothers. . . .*
>
> *Father: you have said that we were in your hand, and that by closing it you could crush us to nothing. Are you determined to crush us? If you are, tell us so, that those of our nation who have become your children, and have determined to die so, may know what to do.*
>
> HALF TOWN, CORNPLANTER, *and* BIG TREE *(Seneca)*, 1790

The Seneca soon found themselves facing another irony. As unfair as the Treaty of Fort Stanwyx had seemed, at least it had promised them that certain lands would be theirs "as long as the sun shall shine and as long as the grass shall grow." Only two decades later, those reserved lands would be threatened and sales of Indian land would further dispossess them.

> *Brother!—Your application for the purchase of our lands is to our minds very extraordinary. It has been made in a crooked manner. You have not walked the straight path pointed out by the great Council of your nation. You have*

no writings from your great Father, the President. In mak-
ing up our minds we have looked back, and remembered
how the Yorkers purchased our lands in former times. They
bought them, piece after piece—for a little money paid to
a few men in our nation, and not to all our brethren—
until our planting and hunting grounds have become very
small, and if we sell them, we know not where to spread
our blankets.

The lands do not belong to the Yorkers; they are ours,
and were given to us by the Great Spirit....

RED JACKET/SAGOYEWATHA *(Seneca)*, 1811

Although the Iroquois did not attempt to prevent the taking
of their lands by warfare, other Indians on the East Coast did.
Among them were the Creek. Part of the Creek nation fought
a Civil War, which became a war of resistance on the part of
the Red Stick Creek against the U.S. government. Other native peoples, including twenty companies of Cherokee and the
White Stick Creek, joined forces with the United States and
fought by the side of General Andrew Jackson. Jackson's life
was saved by his Cherokee allies in the battle of Horseshoe
Bend when the Red Sticks were finally defeated. Jackson
swore everlasting brotherhood to the Cherokee—a brotherhood that would last only until he became president of the
United States and backed the removal of his former allies to
the West.

Your people have destroyed my nation. You are a brave
man. I rely on your generosity. You will exact no terms of
a conquered people, but such as they should accede to.

Whatever they may be, it would be madness and folly to oppose them. If they are opposed, you shall find me among the sternest enforcers of obedience. Those who would still hold out, can be influenced only by a mean spirit of revenge; and, to this, they must not, and shall not, sacrifice the last remnant of their country.

WILLIAM WEATHERFORD/RED EAGLE (*Creek*), 1814

A warrior I have been.
Now
It is all over.
A hard time
I have.

LAST SONG OF SITTING BULL,

date unknown

During the Civil War, Chief Red Cloud had led a coalition of Lakota people in a war against the U.S. Army. After several defeats, the United States agreed to pull out of the contested lands and two U.S. forts were abandoned—and burned to the ground by the victorious Lakota.

Yet the treaties signed with the Sioux were not honored. Although the Black Hills were to be reserved for the Lakota people, white settlers and gold seekers streamed into the Indian lands of the Dakotas after the American Civil War. A road was cut into the heart of Lakota lands by George Armstrong Custer. That road became known to the Indians as the "Thieves' Road."

Seeking justice for his people, that same Chief Red Cloud traveled to visit President Grant.

When you first came we were very many, and you were few; now you are many, and we are getting very few, and we are poor. You do not know who appears before you today to speak. I am a representative of the original American race, the first people of this continent. We are good and not bad....

All I want is right and justice....

Look at me. I am poor and naked, but I am the chief of the Nation. We do not want riches, we do not ask for riches, but we want our children properly trained and brought up. We look to you for your sympathy. Our riches will not do us any good; we cannot take away into the other world anything we have—we want to have peace and love.   RED CLOUD *(Lakota)*, 1870

The Apache were not a single nation, but many different small bands whose homeland was the rugged, dry desert and high mountain landscape of Arizona, New Mexico, and Sierra Madre of Sonora in northern Mexico. Although they tried to live in peace, they were fierce and unrelenting in warfare against those who tried to destroy them—first the Spanish, then the Mexicans, then the Americans who entered their lands in great numbers, seeking silver and gold. It took strong, resilient people to survive in the desert, and the Apache's ability to do so, to run for days without stopping, to see and not be seen, to find food and water where others would starve or die of thirst, made them feared adversaries. A single Apache with a bow and arrows was regarded as more dangerous than a dozen white men with guns. The leaders of their small bands of resistance fighters became known as renegades and murderers, but to their people they were chiefs and patriots. Of the Apache chiefs, the best known among them was surely Cochise.

Famous in war, Cochise was just as renowned in peace as the Apache leader who signed a truce with the U.S. government and saw it honored throughout his lifetime. The following words were spoken to General Gordon Granger during a conference dealing with the plan to send the Chiracahua Apache to a reservation at Tularosa, where Cochise knew it would be hard for his people to survive.

The sun has been very hot on my head and made me as in a fire; my blood was on fire, but now I have come into this valley and drunk of these waters and washed myself in them and they have cooled me. Now that I am cool I have come with my hands open to you to live in peace with you. I speak straight and do not wish to deceive or be deceived. I want a good, strong and lasting peace. When God made the world he gave one part to the white man and another to the Apache....

Now that I am to speak, the sun, the moon, the earth, the air, the waters, the birds and animals, even the children unborn shall rejoice at my words. The white people have looked for me long. I am here....

I do not wish to hide anything from you nor have you hide anything from me; I will not lie to you; do not lie to me. I want to live in these mountains; I do not want to go to Tularosa. That is a long ways off. The flies on those mountains eat out the eyes of the horses. The bad spirits

live there. I have drunk of these waters and they have
cooled me. I do not want to leave here.

COCHISE *(Chiracahua Apache),* 1871

Sitting Bull is one of the most well-known of all American Indians of the last five hundred years. His life is a great American epic, with all the elements of heroism and tragedy. Known to his people not just as a chief and warrior but as a *wicasa wakan,* a holy man whose dreams and visions provided him guidance, he was also a maker of songs. His greatest fame came when his Lakota defeated George Armstrong Custer at the Battle of the Little Big Horn. It was so unthinkable that an American army could be wiped out by mere Indians, as Custer's was, that some newspaper writers in 1876 suggested that Sitting Bull was not really an Indian but a white graduate of West Point, a military genius disguised as a red man.

The Battle of the Little Big Horn, in many ways, can be seen as an act of either great courage or great foolishness on the part of Custer. He was eager to fight a battle in which he would gain glory, some said, because Custer planned to run for president. The timing of the battle was such that newspaper accounts of the expected victory would influence the Republican convention. Custer attacked a huge village of so many Lakota and Cheyenne people that he and his men were greatly outnumbered. In addition, before the attack he broke his force up into three smaller groups, to attack from three sides—as he had done when he wiped out a much smaller Cheyenne and Arapaho village at the Washita some years earlier. An interesting sidelight to this story is that Sitting Bull himself had a vision several days before the white soldiers appeared out of nowhere to attack them at dawn. In the vision, he saw many blue-coated soldiers falling upside down into the Indian camp. He interpreted this as an omen that the Lakota would win a great victory—and they did.

Sitting Bull was a traditional Lakota. After the battle with Custer, known as the Battle of the Little Big Horn, he led his people to sanctuary in Canada and stayed there for a number of years. But he was forced to return to the United States when the buffalo herds his people hunted grew scarce, and he agreed to the Lakota's being placed on a reservation. But Sitting Bull was never a man to be quiet or to accept mistreatment, and he had to face the hostility of the Indian agent in charge of his reservation. Agent McLaughlin disliked Sitting Bull intensely.

Sitting Bull had already become famous and traveled to Europe in Buffalo Bill's Wild West Show. Then came the Ghost Dance. It was a prophetic religious movement begun among the Paiute when a man named Wovoka had a vision. In his vision, he saw that if the people danced in a circle and prayed, the buffalo and all their loved ones would come back. The Lakota began to do the Ghost Dance on the reservation, and feeling this might lead to another uprising, white officials were terrified. McLaughlin set out to punish Sitting Bull and, in December 1890, the agent sent his force of Indian policemen, all of them Lakota, to arrest Sitting Bull. A fight broke out and Sitting Bull was killed.

Sitting Bull, throughout his lifetime, never hesitated to speak his mind. He was often interviewed about the Battle of the Little Big Horn. In one interview he said:

They tell you I murdered Custer. It is a lie. I am not a war chief. I was not in the battle that day. His eyes were blinded that he could not see. He was a fool and he rode to his death. He made the fight, not I. Whoever tells you I killed Yellow Hair is a liar.

SITTING BULL/TATANKA IYOTAKE

(Hunkpapa Lakota), circa 1880

While in Canada in 1877, Sitting Bull made this explanation of why the Lakota were reluctant to fight the whites:

The palefaces had things that we needed in order to hunt. We needed ammunition. Our interests were in peace. I never sold that much land. [Here Sitting Bull picked up with his thumb and forefinger a little dirt, lifted it, and let it fall and blow away.] I never made or sold a treaty with the United States. I came in to claim my rights and the rights of my people, I was driven in force from my land. I never made war on the United States Government. I never stood in the white man's country. I never committed any depredations in the white man's country. I never made the white man's heart bleed. The white man came on my land and followed me. The white man made me fight for my hunting grounds. The white man made me kill him or he would kill my friends, my women, and my children.

We have all fought hard. We did not know Custer. There was not as many Indians as the white man says. There was not more than two thousand. I did not want to kill any more men. I did not like that kind of work. I only defended my camp. When we had killed enough, that was all that was necessary.

SITTING BULL/TATANKA IYOTAKE *(Hunkpapa Lakota)*, 1877

For seven decades, the Nez Perce of the beautiful Wallowa Valley in eastern Oregon had been the friends and allies of the Americans. No Nez Perce had ever injured or killed a white man. In 1873, President Grant had issued an executive order that the Nez Perce of the Wallowa Valley would never have to give up their lands. Then, as had happened with the Cherokee and the Lakota Sioux, gold was discovered on their lands. The Nez Perce, under the leadership of men such as Chief Joseph and the prophet Toohoolhoolzote, were told that they must sell their homes and move to a reservation. But the Nez Perce did not see the land the same way white men did. Selling the land would be the same as selling themselves. Like the other native peoples of the continent, the land and the people were one.

"The earth is part of our body and we never gave up the earth," Toohoolhoolzote said at the time. "We came from the earth and our bodies must go back to the earth, our mother."

Chief Joseph told of the moving last words spoken to him by his father, Old Joseph:

My father sent for me. I saw he was dying. I took his hand in mine. He said: "My son, my body is returning to my mother earth, and my spirit is going very soon to see the Great Spirit Chief. When I am gone, think of your country. You are the chief of these people. They took to you to guide them. Always remember that your father never sold his country. You must stop your ears whenever you are asked to sign a treaty selling your home. A few years more, and white men will be all around you. They have their eyes on this land. My son, never forget my dying words. This country holds your father's body. Never sell the bones of your father and your mother." I pressed my father's hand and told him I would protect his grave with my life. My father smiled and passed away to the spirit-land.

I buried him in that beautiful valley of winding waters. I love that land more than all the rest of the world. A man who would not love his father's grave is worse than a wild animal.

CHIEF JOSEPH/IN-MUT-TOO-YAH-LAT-LAT *(Nez Perce)*, 1879

But all the eloquent arguments of the Nez Perce, the staunch friends of the white men, were of no avail. Speaking of those negotiations, Chief Joseph would later say:

The white men were many and we could not hold our own with them. We were like deer. They were like grizzly bears. We had a small country. Their country was large. We were contented to let things remain as the Great Spirit made them. They were not, and would change the rivers and mountains if they did not suit them.

CHIEF JOSEPH/IN-MUT-TOO-YAH-LAT-LAT *(Nez Perce)*, 1879

Till the day of his death in 1904, Chief Joseph kept speaking for his people.

My friends, I have been asked to show you my heart. I am glad to have a chance to do so. I want the white people to understand my people. Some of you think an Indian is like a wild animal. This is a great mistake. I will tell you all about our people, and then you can judge whether an Indian is a man or not. I believe much trouble and blood would be saved if we opened our hearts more. I will tell you in my way how the Indian sees things. The white man has more words to tell you how they look to him, but it does not require many words to speak the truth. What I have to say will come from my heart, and I will speak with a straight tongue. Ah-cum-kin-i-ma-me-hut [the Great Spirit Chief] is looking at me and will hear me.

My name is In-mut-too-yah-lat-lat (Thunder Traveling over the Mountains). I am chief of the Wal-lam-wat-kin back of Chute-pa-lu, or Nez Perces [nose-pierced Indians]. I was born in eastern Oregon, thirty-eight winters ago. My father was chief before me. He died a few years ago. When a young man, he was called Joseph by Mr. Spaulding, a missionary. He left us a good name on earth. He advised me well for my people.

Our fathers gave us many laws, which they had learned from their fathers. These laws were good. They told us to treat all men as they treated us; that we should never be the first to break a bargain; that it was a disgrace to tell a lie; that it was a shame for one man to take from another his wife, or his property without paying for it. We were taught to believe that the Great Spirit sees and hears everything, and that he never forgets; that hereafter he will give every man a spirit-home according to his deserts: if he has been a good man, he will have a good home; if he has been a bad man, he will have a bad home. This I believe, and all my people believe the same....

If the white man wants to live in peace with the Indian he can live in peace. There need be no trouble. Treat all men alike. Give them the same law. Give them all an equal chance to live and grow. All men were made by the same Great Spirit Chief. They are all brothers. The earth is the mother of all people, and all people should have equal rights upon it. You might as well expect the rivers to run backward as that any man who was born a free man should be contented when penned up and denied liberty to go where he pleases. . . .

Whenever the white man treats an Indian as they treat each other, then we will have no more wars. Then shall all be alike—brothers of one father and one mother, with one sky above us and one country around us, and one government for all. Then the Great Spirit Chief who rules above will smile upon this land and send rain to wash out the bloody spots made by brothers' hands from the face of the earth. For this time the Indian race are waiting and praying. I hope that no more groans of wounded men and women will ever go to the ear of the Great Spirit Chief above, and that all people may be one people.

In-mut-too-yah-lat-lat has spoken for his people.

CHIEF JOSEPH/IN-MUT-TOO-YAH-LAT-LAT (*Nez Perce*), 1879

One of the most feared of Indian warriors, the man known to most as Geronimo, evaded capture by an army of more than five thousand troops before his final surrender in 1886, even though he led only a handful of other warriors. Born in 1829, even in his fifties he was one of the most feared Indians in history.

Not a chief, but a medicine man and war leader, it was said

that Geronimo could predict the future. The power he carried with him would speak to him and tell him how to avoid capture. He was told by his power that no bullet or arrow would ever kill him. Despite enduring more than four decades of warfare against the Mexicans, who slaughtered his family, and the Americans, who took away his homeland, he would die of pneumonia at the age of eighty in the military hospital at Fort Sill.

I have several times asked for peace, but trouble has come from the agents and interpreters. I don't want what has passed to happen again. Now, I am going to tell you something else. The Earth-Mother is listening to me and I hope that all may be arranged that from now on there shall be no trouble and that we shall always have peace.... From now on I do not want that anything shall be told you about me even in joke. Whenever I have broken out it has always been on account of bad talk. From this day on I hope that people will tell me nothing but the truth....

There is one God looking down on us all. We are all children of the one God. God is listening to me. The sun, the darkness, the winds, are all listening to what we say.

GERONIMO/GOYATHLAY *(Bedonkohe Apache)*, 1886

Geronimo lived out the rest of his life in captivity at Fort Sill. Even after his death in 1909, his body was not sent back to his beloved Apache lands. Instead, he was buried on the military firing range in Oklahoma. Feared by his enemies and described by the press as a bloodthirsty villain during his life, today he is remembered as a hero, a man who always fought for the freedom of his people.

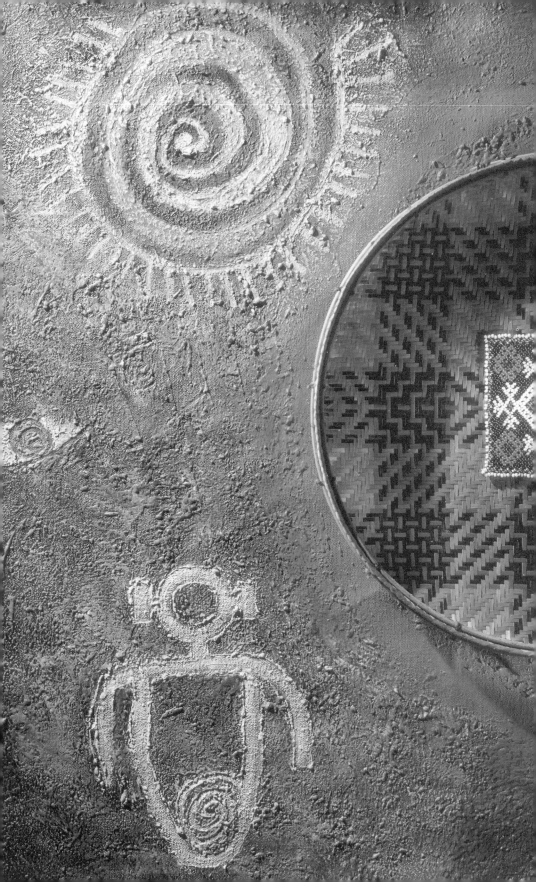

5. WALKING NEW ROADS

I want my people

to live like white people

and have the same chance ...

We want to travel

the same road

as the white man.

LITTLE RAVEN (*Arapaho*), 1871

THERE HAVE long been many voices and many visions among Native Americans. It is especially interesting to hear some of those voices from the time when it seemed as if the Indian was either going to vanish or become just like the whites. Some were able to walk the new road between the white and Indian worlds. Their own words illustrate their experience with the growing dominance of the white culture.

Although many Europeans were willing to adopt Indian

ways and traditions, it was not as easy for Indians to live white lives. Even being educated in the white man's school was something about which Indian people held divided opinions. Such schools did not merely teach their Indian students European American culture; they almost always asked that the Native Americans give up their own cultures and religious traditions in exchange for those of the European. Conversion to Christianity was usually a requirement for any American Indian student in the 1600s and 1700s. By the mid-1700s, a number of Native Americans in the Northeast had actually gained university educations, usually as divinity students.

However, when in 1774 the Iroquois were offered the opportunity to send boys as students to William and Mary College, they declined.

> *But you, who are wise, must know that different nations have different conceptions of things and you will not therefore take it amiss, if our ideas of this kind of education happen not to be the same as yours. We have had some experience of it. Several of our young people were formerly brought up at the colleges of the northern provinces; they were instructed in all your sciences, but when they came back to us, they were bad runners, ignorant of every means of living in the woods, unable to bear either cold or hunger, knew neither how to build a cabin or take a deer, spoke our language imperfectly, were therefore neither fit for hunters, warriors, nor counsellors; they were totally good for nothing.*
>
> *We are, however, not the less obliged by your kind*

offer, though we decline accepting it; and, to show our grateful sense of it, if the gentlemen of Virginia will send us a dozen of their sons, we will take care of their education, instruct them in all we know, and make men *of them.* UNIDENTIFIED IROQUOIS, 1774

From the time of first contact with the Europeans, there were always Native Americans who chose to attempt to walk the white man's road. Some of those attempts ended in tragedy, yet a surprising number of their stories are tales of triumph. It was never easy, but there were usually some Native Americans who successfully lived within the culture of the newcomers, spoke their languages, dressed as they dressed, and followed their ways. Yet even when they seemed most "white," like Samson Occom, who became a Christian minister in the mid-1700s, their first loyalties almost always remained with their native people.

The life of Samson Occom is both the epic of an incredible journey of faith and an early example of a European-educated Native American who found out how difficult it was to follow the white man's way. Even his birth name hints at the task he would undertake. In Mohegan, *occom* means "the other side."

Throughout his adult life, Samson Occom kept a daily journal. He tells in it how he lived in his native Connecticut in the old Mohegan way when he was a child:

"My parents lived a wandering life. They chiefly depended upon hunting, fishing and fowling for their living and had no connection with the English, excepting to traffic with them in their small trifles."

Mohegan life was not without cares. Earthly existence in

the dominant culture sometimes seemed to hold little or no promise for the Indian. One day, the words Samson Occom heard spoken about Christ by a minister, probably from New London, touched the young man's spirit and he was converted to Christianity at the age of seventeen.

"From this time the distress and burden of my mind was removed, and I found serenity and pleasure of soul, in serving God," he said.

Occom began to study with Reverend Eleazar Wheelock. Occom was a brilliant student. He studied Greek and Latin, Hebrew, the Scriptures, and music. He particularly loved singing and began a lifelong study of hymns and spiritual songs. He also acted as a spiritual counselor to the Mohegan. Wheelock's success with Occom, his first Indian student, was so impressive that it was easy for Wheelock to find backers for an institution to train Indians—Moor's Indian Charity School.

By the time Occom was twenty-seven, he was appointed to be the minister, schoolmaster, and interpreter for the Montauk Indians of Long Island. There he met a Montauk woman named Mary Fowler, who became his wife. His pay as schoolmaster and minister was only fifteen pounds a year. An unmarried white minister doing the same work would have received four times as much. Within a few years, Occom had not only himself, but a large household to support; he and Mary had six children. In the Mohegan way, Occom spent whatever money he earned not only on himself and his immediate family, but on the Indian community around him. Despite the poor pay, Occom stayed with the Montauk for twelve years. To survive, Occom supplemented his income by farming, hunting, and fishing, and working as a skilled artisan.

"I used to be out hoeing my corn sometimes before sunrise and after my school is dismissed.... At other times I bound old books for Easthampton people, made wooden spoons and ladles, stocked guns and worked on cedar to make pails, piggins and churns," he wrote.

At the request of a missionary organization that he work with the Oneida people, Occom began in the 1760s to travel to the West. Two decades later, he would lead a large contingent of his Mohegan people to form a Christian Indian community called Brothertown on Oneida lands in 1784 accompanied by his brother-in-law, David Fowler.

It was now becoming more and more evident to Occom that he was not being treated fairly. He knew the pay that non-Indians received for the sort of work he did.

> *I was my own interpreter. I was both a school master and minister to the Indians, yea I was their ear, eye and hand, as well as mouth. I leave it to the World, as wicked as it is, to judge, whether I ought not to have had half as much. But I must say, "I believe it is, because I am a poor Indian."* SAMSON OCCOM *(Mohegan)*, 1764

In 1764, the trouble the Mohegan people were having with the white people who claimed Indian land worsened. All of their lands, except for five thousand acres, were granted to Connecticut. Such treatment of the Indians lead Occom to the conclusion that moving west was the only solution.

> *I am afraid the poor Indian will never stand a chance against the English in their land controversies because they*

are very poor, they have no money. Money is almighty now-adays and the Indians have no learning, no wit, no cunning, the English have it all.

SAMSON OCCOM (*Mohegan*), 1764

Meanwhile, Reverend Wheelock was having financial difficulties and decided to appeal to supporters in England, where many sympathized with the plight of the Indian. He chose two ministers, one white, one Indian, as emissaries to travel to the British Isles. Reverend Nathaniel Whitaker was one. Reverend Samson Occom was the other. The money, Occom was told, would be used for the education of Indians. It was a cause his soul embraced. Leaving his beloved family behind, he set off on his great journey.

For two and a half years, Whitaker and Occom traveled throughout England and Scotland. Huge crowds came to their meetings, to see the Indian minister. They raised a small fortune, more than twelve thousand pounds. People loved Occom. Wheelock, however, in his letters to Occom, criticized his protégé for becoming too proud.

On his return to America, Occom found that none of the money he had worked to raise was to be used for Indian education. Despite Wheelock's promises to the Indians and the support of the many donors who gave so freely, Wheelock turned his back on Occom and the Indians. The funds were used to turn Moor's Indian Charity School into a new institution, one for non-Indian students. That school was Dartmouth College. All that remained of its original identity as a school for Native Americans was the name "Indians," which is still the name of Dartmouth sports teams to this day.

For several years, Occom was adrift. Without a salary and in poor health, he turned again to his Mohegan people, seeking to help them in their own dark hours.

Eventually, Occom found his way back. In 1772, the Boston Board of Commissioners of the Congregational Church restored his salary. In 1774, pursuing his lifelong love of music, Occom published a hymnal: *A Choice Collection of Hymns and Spiritual Songs Intended for the Edification of Sincere Christians of All Denominations.* That same year, Occom began assisting seven of the Indian communities of southern New England to form a new community with land obtained from neighboring Oneida people. Brothertown was successfully completed in 1784.

Few ministers of his time enjoyed the popularity of Samson Occom. Not only his own Mohegan people, but also the Montauk, the Oneida, and numerous other native peoples of the Northeast viewed him as a spiritual leader, as did many of the English on both sides of the Atlantic. Perhaps part of the reason for that popularity can be found in his own words.

> *Live in peace. Cultivate peace. Take care to plant, manure, and cherish it as ye vintner his vine, or ye husbandman his corn.*   SAMSON OCCOM *(Mohegan),* date unknown

There is no official record of the birth of William Apess and no record of his death. Had it not been for his own writings, his life would not be known. His parents, he wrote, were Pequot. To be Pequot in 1798 meant that you were survivors of a people whose eradication from the earth had been attempted—with some success—in 1637 by the Puritans. The treaty signed by the few Pequot survivors of the 1637 massacre declared them extinct and banned forever the use of the name Pequot. Even as late as 1798, calling yourself a Pequot was a risky thing to do in New England. Disheartened, poverty-stricken, stripped of culture and pride, such people as Apess's elders were people who saw no pride in their past, no hope in the present, and little or no chance in the future.

Left along with his brothers and sisters in the hands of abusive grandparents, Apess was "bound out"—sold into a form of slavery until he reached adulthood. Frequently "bound out" servants were Native American children. In return for their labor, the bound servants were given food and clothes, a place to stay, and a small amount of education. Apess ran away from his masters more than once. In 1809, as a small boy, he began attending Methodist meetings and converted to Christianity. He became a Methodist preacher in 1820.

In 1829, Apess became the first American Indian to publish an autobiography, *A Son of the Forest*. In 1833, while working with the Mashpee Indians of the Massachussetts coast, he became a strong advocate for their rights and was involved in the "Mashpee Revolt." He was fined and jailed for a month— for disturbing the peace—as a result of his speeches. In 1836, he delivered his most famous speech, the "Eulogy on King Philip." In 1838, he disappeared and was never seen again.

William Apess's life blazed a brief trail across the sky and then vanished. It is to Apess's everlasting credit that he began to turn that tide of slander, to speak as an educated Native American for his contemporaries and for the generations to come.

In his autobiography, Apess includes the following truly

poignant story of how he, as an Indian child, was made to be afraid of his own people:

One day, several of the family went into the woods to gather berries, taking me with them. We had not been out long before we fell in with a company of white females, on the same errand—their complexion was, to say the least, as dark as that of natives. This circumstance filled my mind with terror, and I broke from the party with my utmost speed, and I could not muster courage enough to look behind until I had reached home. By this time my imagination had pictured out a tale of blood, and as soon as I regained breath to answer the questions which my master asked, I informed him that we had met a party of natives in the woods, but what became of the party I could not tell. . . .

It may be proper for me here to remark that the great fear I entertained of my brethren was occasioned by the many stories I had heard of their cruelty toward the whites—how they were in the habit of killing and scalping men, women and children. But the whites did not tell me that they were in a great majority of instances the aggressors—that they had imbrued their hands in the lifeblood of my brethren, driven them from their once peaceful and happy homes—that they introduced among them the fatal exterminating diseases of civilized life.

WILLIAM APESS (*Pequot*), 1829

By the early 1800s, the Seneca people had decided that it was necessary for a few of their young men to get a white education in order to be able to help their people. Ely Parker, whose Indian name as a child was Ha-sa-no-an-da—which might be translated as either "Leading Name" or "The Open Book"—was one of those chosen. At first he was an indifferent student. But when a group of white men ridiculed his broken English, he vowed that no one would ever make fun of his ability to speak again, and threw himself into his studies. He became fluent not only in English, but in Greek and Latin. By the age of sixteen he was famous as an orator. At Cayuga Academy, people filled the lecture hall whenever he spoke.

Much of his time in his teenage years and twenties, when not in school, was spent representing his Seneca people, whose remaining lands in New York State were being taken illegally. He became known to the New York governors and met with four succeeding presidents of the United States. Parker's efforts were largely responsible for the Seneca successfully resisting removal. They were able to hold on to much of their land at Tonawanda, which remains a Seneca Reservation up to this day. In 1851, at the age of twenty-three, Parker was chosen by the women of his clan to become a chief, a grand sachem, and took on the name of Donehogawa—"Guardian of the Western Door."

Despite his role as a grand sachem, Parker did not give up his life in the white world. He was employed by the U.S. government as a civil engineer, and befriended Ulysses S. Grant while working in Grant's hometown of Galena, Illinois. When the Civil War came, Grant made Parker his personal secretary, making him a brevet general. "The Big Indian," as the soldiers called him, was by Grant's side throughout the latter part of the American Civil War. At Appomattox, Parker wrote down the terms of General Lee's surrender. Shaking Parker's hand, Lee said, "I am glad to see there is one real American here." Parker responded, "We are all Americans here."

After the war, Ely Parker joined President Grant's administration as the first American Indian Commissioner of Indian Affairs. His efforts to end the corruption in the Indian Bureau, firing dishonest agents and replacing them with Quakers, made him enemies. In 1871, Parker was forced to resign, after having successfully pursued—for the first time in American history—a peace policy with the Indians on the part of the United States. Parker's influence had led to the treaty with Red Cloud and his Lakota, and prevented a number of armed conflicts between Indians and whites during his term of office. He also brought an end to the practice of making unfair treaties with Indian tribes, treaties always broken by the whites.

Had Parker remained in office, would the policy of wiping out the buffalo herds have been put into place? Would the tragic wars against the Modoc and Apache, the Cheyenne and Kiowa and Comanche, the Sioux and Nez Perce have been prevented? Would Custer have died at Little Big Horn? Would the Ghost Dance dreams of the Lakota have ended in the bloody snows of Wounded Knee? No one will ever know.

Few Americans were as influential in their time as Ely Parker—in both Indian and white worlds. Civil War General and Grand Sachem of the Iroquois, Commissioner of Indian Affairs and advocate for his Seneca people. Ely Parker's story is an inspiring one. A hundred years would pass before any Indian would hold any office as high as Ely Parker held in

Grant's administration. Until the second half of the twentieth century, when a new generation of Native American lawyers would begin to gain justice in the courts of America, there would be few victories like those Ely Parker won.

The isolated world of the western Paiute people of Sarah Winnemucca was far removed from that of Ely Parker's Iroquois, who had been dealing with Europeans for centuries. Sarah Winnemucca's childhood, when she quite literally feared the white people would come to eat her and her family, could not have been more different from her adult life, when she found herself traveling across the United States, speaking on behalf of her people. Her 1883 volume, *Life among the Piutes,* would be the first book about Native Americans by a Native American woman.

Her people, the northern Paiute, lived in western Nevada. Her mother, Tuboitonie, and her father, Winnemucca, gave her the Paiute name Thocmetony, which means "Shellflower." Sarah Winnemucca allowed herself to be described at her lectures as an "Indian Princess," because she knew it would attract white audiences. Her people lived quite democratically in small bands of relatives. As she wrote in her book:

> *The chiefs do not rule like tyrants; they discuss everything with their people, as a father would with his family. Often they sit up all night. They discuss the doings of all, if they need to be advised.... If the women are interested they can share in the talks.... The women sit behind them in another circle, and if the children wish to hear, they can be there too.*

The women know as much as the men do, and their advice is often asked. . . . They are always interested in what their husbands are doing and thinking about. And they take part even in the wars. . . . It means something when the women promise their fathers to make their husbands themselves. They faithfully keep with them in all the danger they share. They not only take care of their children together, but they do everything together.

SARAH WINNEMUCCA *(Paiute)*, 1883

The expedition of John Charles Frémont in 1844, the year of Sarah's birth, first brought white men into northern Paiute lands. The Paiute welcomed Frémont and his twenty-five men with the greeting *"truckee, truckee,"* which might be translated as "all is good." Frémont treated them with courtesy. Among those dozen men who greeted Frémont and his party was one of the leaders of the Paiute who Frémont called "Captain Truckee." Captain Truckee and a dozen of Frémont's new Paiute friends traveled with him to California, returning home with new clothes, guns, and ammunition. Truckee was Sarah Winnemucca's grandfather. When he spoke to his little granddaughter, she later recalled, he often "said I must not be afraid of the white people, for they are very good. I told him they looked so very bad I could not help it."

The next Paiute impression of white men was more ominous. A party of eighty-seven California-bound settlers became lost and snowbound in the Sierra Nevada in 1846. Those white settlers, the Donner party, turned to murder and cannibalism of their own people. Forty-seven members of the Donner party survived and their story spread throughout the West. Hearing this horrified the Paiute. They began to wonder if all whites, with their large eyes and white faces as pale as those of the owls, were cannibals. They also heard that whites were killing Indians for no reason. From then on, the first impulse of many Paiute was to run and hide whenever they heard that whites were coming. Sarah Winnemucca described one such occasion as her aunt and her mother concealed her and her cousin when they were fleeing from a group of whites and the little girls would not keep up with them.

> *"Let us bury our girls or we shall all be killed and eaten up." So they went to work and buried us, and told us if we heard any noise not to cry out, for if we did (the white people) would surely kill us and eat us. So our mothers buried me and my cousin, planted sage bushes over our faces to keep the sun from burning them, and there we were left all day.*
>
> *Oh, can anyone imagine my feelings buried alive, thinking every minute that I was to be unburied by the people that my grandfather loved so much.... At last we heard some whispering.... I could hear their footsteps coming nearer and nearer. I thought my heart was coming out of my mouth. Then I heard my mother say, "'Tis right here!" Oh, can anyone in the world ever imagine what were my feelings when I was dug up by my poor mother and father?* SARAH WINNEMUCCA (*Paiute*), 1883

Despite her grandfather's reassuring words, her first meeting with white people terrified her:

My mother said there were two white men coming.

"Oh, mother, what shall I do? Hide me!" I just danced around like a wild one. . . . I was behind my mother. When they were coming nearer, I heard my grandfather say "Make a place for them to sit down."

Just then I peeped round my mother to see them. I gave one scream, and said, "Oh, mother, the owls!"

I only saw their big white eyes, and I thought their faces were all hair. My mother said, "I wish you would send your brothers away, for my child will die."

I imagined I could see their big white eyes all night long. They were the first ones I had ever seen in my life.

SARAH WINNEMUCCA *(Paiute),* 1883

In 1857, when she was thirteen, Sarah and her sister Elma went to live with the Ormsby family in Genoa. There she recalled "we learned the English language very fast, for they were very kind to us." Between 1858 and 1861, she and Elma continued their education as students at the Convent of Notre Dame in San Jose, until they were forced to leave because of white objections about their presence.

Over the next few decades, things grew more difficult for the Paiute. The discovery of gold in California and silver in Nevada drew in more and more prospectors and settlers. Great numbers of white people came into what had been Indian land. Even the areas eventually set aside by the government as reservation lands for the Paiute were infringed upon by dangerous, armed white men who believed that killing Indians was the right thing to do. Some Paiute, both men and women, were committed to fight. They would do so with courage and skill, winning more than one victory but losing the war eventually against the more numerous and better armed whites.

In 1870, Sarah Winnemucca brought herself to the attention of the wider public for the first time when she wrote a letter to the new Indian Superintendent for Nevada about the hard time her people were having. The letter became the talk of Washington, D.C., and was published in *Harper's Weekly*. It was the beginning of a life in the public eye. Between 1870 and 1883, she traveled around the nation speaking on behalf of her people.

The *Daily Alta California* reported these words from one of her speeches:

> *I want homes for my people but no one will help us. I call upon white people in their private homes. They will not touch my fingers for fear of getting soiled. . . .*
>
> *You take all the natives of the earth in your bosom but the poor Indian, who is born of your land and who lived for generations on the land which the good God has given to them, and you say he must be exterminated. You say he must be exterminated. You say he must be exterminated.*
>
> *The proverb says the big fish eat up the little fish and we Indians are the little fish and you eat us up and drive us from home.* SARAH WINNEMUCCA (*Paiute*), 1883

In 1885, with the help of such eastern philanthropists as Elizabeth O. Peabody and with the money earned from her book and her lectures, Sarah Winnemucca opened a school for Paiute children in Nevada. Sarah Winnemucca's idea was too far ahead of its time to succeed. It would only be in the second half of the twentieth century that Indian-run schools would again take up the educational challenge that Sarah Winnemucca met in her life—remaining immersed in her own culture and her people while learning the language and the ways of the mainstream.

> *If I were a pony*
> *A spotted pinto pony,*
> *A racing, running pinto pony,*
> *I would run away from school.*
> *And I'd gallop on the mesa,*
> *And I'd eat on the mesa,*
> *And I'd sleep on the mesa,*
> *And I'd never think of school.*
>
> GROUP POEM BY NAVAJO STUDENTS AT
> THE TOHATCHI SCHOOL, NEW MEXICO, 1933

In the period between 1870 and 1970, Indian boarding schools became a dominant feature of Indian life. Native American children were taken away without the permission of their tribal communities or their families—sometimes by force. They were shipped off to distant places, often more than a thousand miles from home. There they were dressed in military uniforms, forced to cut their hair short, and harshly disciplined if they spoke their native language. Many died there—if not of disease then of loneliness and broken hearts.

> *You want our children to go to the schools that you have*
> *for us. Do you come to our old people first and tell us*
> *about the schools, and explain to us what the schools are*

for, so that we may understand? We Indians only know that schools will make our children like white people, and some of us, some of us do not like white people and their ways.

Of course I know that schools are good and that white people mean them to help our people. Schools are good; it is right for everyone to learn all he can from everyone. But white people should be more gentle with the older Indians if we cannot understand. Our lives are sad—and we love our children. If I came to take your children to some strange place to learn things of which you knew nothing, would you like it? If I, an Indian woman, took your children into the desert to make them grow like Indians, would you like it? We Indians have the same love for our brown children that you have for your white ones. . . . CHIPAROPAI *(Yuma),* 1920

Luther Standing Bear, who became well-known as an author and spokesperson for his people in the early 1900s, was one of the first of his generation to be sent off to a boarding school. His description of his arrival at Carlisle in 1879, when he was eleven years old, is poignant.

At that time I thought nothing of it, but I now realize that I was the first Indian boy to step inside the Carlisle Indian School grounds.

Here the girls were all called to one side by Louise McCoz, the girls' interpreter. She took them into one of the big buildings, which was very brilliantly lighted, and it looked good to us from the outside. . . .

But the room we entered was empty. A cast-iron stove

stood in the middle of the room, on which was placed a coal-oil lamp. There was no fire in the stove. We ran through all the rooms, but they were all the same—no fire, no beds. This was a two-story building, but we were all herded into two rooms on the upper floor.

Well, we had to make the best of the situation, so we took off our leggins and rolled them up for a pillow. All the covering we had was the blanket we each had brought. We went to sleep on the hard floor, and it was cold. We had been used to sleeping on the ground, but the floor was so much colder.

Next morning we were called downstairs for breakfast. All we were given was bread and water. How disappointed we were. At noon we had some meat, bread, and coffee, so we felt a little better. But how lonesome the big boys and girls were for their faraway Dakota homes where there was plenty to eat! The big boys seemed to take it worse than we smaller chaps did. I guess we little fellows did not know any better. The big boys would sing brave songs, and that would start the girls to crying. They did this for several nights. The girls' quarters were about a hundred and fifty yards from ours, so we could hear them crying. After some time the food began to get better, but it was far from being what we had been used to receiving back home.

LUTHER STANDING BEAR (*Lakota*), 1928

A Santa Clara Pueblo woman's memories of the day she was taken to the Santa Fe Indian School were painfully vivid in 1915.

I remember it was in October and we had a pile of red chile and we were tying chiles into fours. And then my grandfather was putting them on a longer string. We were doing that when they came to get me. Then right away my grandma and my mother started to cry. "Her? She's just a little girl! She's just a little girl, you can't take her."

"But we have to take somebody. We can't take your grandson, so we have to take your granddaughter...."

The next day my mother sent me...to the relatives' houses to be blessed, where they are always sending us when we are leaving our village. They used to send us to relatives to be blessed so that the Creator can take care of us when we are away from our families....

My mother put her best shawl on me. It was getting a little chilly. It was late. Pretty soon the train whistled around the bend near the Rio Grande and it came. I was already five years old, but my grandpa was holding me on his knee. So when the train came, I got in. I saw the tears coming out of that brave man, my grandpa who was so brave and strong.

I can still picture my folks to this day, just standing there crying, and I was missing them....

ANONYMOUS *(Santa Clara)*, 1915

At the boarding schools, there was often not enough food for the children to eat. One Apache boy's memories in 1925 of his experiences at the Santa Fe Indian School centered around that hunger.

Classes would let out at maybe four o'clock and we wouldn't eat until five or five thirty. And when we had some time there, we were all so hungry. We were just little boys.

They used to feed the horses. Besides alfalfa, they fed them corn and bran. The shelled corn. We used to go in there and take the shelled corn and go back there by the arroyo and find a piece of roofing tin, build a fire under it, and parch corn. I just got used to eating parched corn that way. Some of the kids who were smart, they'd take the bran and mix it with water . . . and make little patties, little tortillas of bran. UNIDENTIFIED APACHE BOY, 1925

Not all boarding school experiences were bad. Many students came to value the education they received. By the 1930s, changes in U.S. Indian policy began to allow native students the right to speak in their own languages while at boarding school. The Santa Fe Indian School became nationally known for its policy of encouraging its students to pursue the arts, and the surrounding Pueblo saw it as a community school. Although it was closed by the U.S. government in 1962, the All-Pueblo Indian Council reopened it as a tribally run school in 1981.

Mountain Wolf Woman enjoyed her time at Indian schools in the 1890s. She was a teenager in the Lutheran Mission School in Wittenberg, Wisconsin, when her education came to a sudden end.

They took me out of school. Alas, I was enjoying school so much and they made me stop. They took me back home. They had let me go to school and now they made me quit. It was then that they told me I was going to be married. I cried but it did not do any good. What would my crying avail me? They had already arranged it.

MOUNTAIN WOLF WOMAN *(Winnebago)*, 1961

Few of the Plains Indian leaders better exemplify the way of walking between the white and Indian worlds than Quanah Parker. His mother, Cynthia Ann Parker, was taken captive by the Comanche in May of 1836 in the Navasota River area of Texas, when she was nine years old. She literally became a Comanche herself, and was the wife of Peta Nocona, a war chief of the Quahada (Antelope) band of Comanche. Her son, Quanah, was born sometime around 1852. When Quanah was nine years old, his mother and her youngest child, a girl named Prairie Flower, were captured by Texas Rangers and returned to their white relatives. She had lived as a Comanche for twenty-five years and was heartbroken at being taken from her adopted people, her husband, and her sons. A few years later, Quanah's father and then his aunt, who had adopted him as a foster son, died. Perhaps self-conscious of his mixed ancestry, he tried to be more Comanche than any of the other young men. He distinguished himself as a fearless warrior in raids against white settlements on Comanche lands and the buffalo hunters who were destroying the herds that fed his people. But when he at last surrendered in 1875 at Fort Sill, leading a band of warriors, one of his first questions concerned the whereabouts of his mother and little sister. Colonel Mackenzie, who admired the intelligence, the bravery, and the love of family shown by the young Comanche, wrote a letter for Quanah about his mother and sister that was published in a Dallas newspaper. Soon after it was published, Quanah learned that his little sister and mother had both died.

Quanah then embarked on his second life, a life as a leader of the Comanche along a new path. It was a path where following the white man's way, yet still remaining Indian, would be his main goal. He would counsel peace, yet defend his people's rights, urge young Comanche to gain education, yet follow Native American religious practices. He would live to be, among whites, one of the most respected Indians in the West, and his words reflect his wisdom.

I am related to both the white and the Indian people. I realize it as so, and for that reason will not do anything bad, but looking for the good road, a suppliant for the red people, so when Washington hears he will help us.

QUANAH PARKER *(Comanche)*, 1881

I hear the Kiowa and Cheyennes say there are Indians come from heaven and want me to take my people and go to see them. But I tell them that I want my people to work and pay no attention to that. We depend on the government to help us and not them.

QUANAH PARKER *(Comanche)*, 1890

I have talked to these Indians about making their own living, and to live like white men. I keep my own people straight. It is what you want at Washington to keep the people straight.   QUANAH PARKER *(Comanche)*, 1892

Do not go at this thing like you were riding a swift horse, but hold up a little.   QUANAH PARKER *(Comanche)*, 1892

I have told all the Secretaries and Commissioners that if anything was done to open up our country for settlement, the Government should see to it that more land per capita be given us because our country is not a good farming country and we would have to get our supplies from raising cattle.   QUANAH PARKER *(Comanche)*, 1895

Tell the president that the buffalo is my old friend, and it would make my heart glad to see a herd once more roaming around Mount Scott.   QUANAH PARKER *(Comanche)*, 1907

Although he had his rivals among his people, the majority of the other Comanche acknowledged this leading role played by Quanah, both by supporting his positions and by speaking highly of him, as did Eschiti (Wolf Rump), the Comanche medicine man at that same meeting in 1892 when Eschiti said: "Quanah has things, as it were, written on his tongue. What he learns from the Government he writes on his tongue and we learn from him."

Admiration for Quanah Parker was not limited among Indians. Apache John, a tribal leader of the Kiowa-Apache, while part of a delegation to a Washington Senate Committee meeting on Indian Affairs in March of 1898, said this about Quanah: "Those people who came here a short time ago may have told you that Quanah is a bad man; but I know better; he is just like light, you strike a match in a dark room and there is light; that is the way with Quanah, wherever he is, is light."

Quanah constantly spoke of the need for his people to gain education. Many of his own children went to Indian boarding schools, such as the famous one at Carlisle where Mesquakie Indian Jim Thorpe played football in a later decade. One of Quanah's numerous trips east to speak for his people took him, in 1896, both to Washington and to Carlisle, where several of his children were students. At Carlisle he spoke these words:

> *I do not talk English very much. I been here four days. I look at all you. I find everything good. I come two thousand miles west. Oklahoma, that's where I come from. Telegraph to commissioner, me want to see my children. I go down Washington. I tell what I see here. Government wants to open the Indian country. Indian he no ready yet, maybe half of it, they ready. That's what I come for. That's what I tell commissioner.* QUANAH PARKER (*Comanche*), 1896

Some years later, in 1908, Quanah would speak to the Comanche County superintendent of schools, arguing that another school district be established for both white and Indian students in his area. Without such a school, Quanah's children were forced to go to an extremely poor school for Indians only at Fort Sill. "No like Indian school for my people. Indian boy go to Indian school, stay like Indian; go white school, he like white man. Me want white school so my children get educated like whites...."

Quanah ended up as president of the new district school board.

By the time Quanah died in 1911, he had completed a most remarkable journey. He had gone from being a warrior, raiding white settlements, to being a cattleman with a telephone in his house and a community leader praised in public by President Theodore Roosevelt as a good citizen. His legacy amounted to more than just the town in Texas named after him and the cattle ranch he successfully ran: His life was vivid evidence that an intelligent Native American could survive the changes forced upon his people and compete with the whites on equal terms. Like Samson Occom of the Mohegan, Ely Parker of the Seneca, and Sarah Winnemucca of the Paiute, he had proven it possible for an Indian to straddle two worlds and succeed in both.

Yet the last word about the necessity of learning the ways of the whites belongs, in my mind, to the man who was known for his opposition to the Europeanization of the Indian—Sitting Bull. Invited to speak to the Lakota children on his reservation who were attending a Catholic school, Sitting Bull did not encourage those children to give up being Indian, but, as always, stressed the importance of being able to learn new ways to defend their people.

My dear grandchildren: All of your folks are my relatives, because I am a Sioux, and so are they. I was glad to hear that the Black Robe had given you this school where you can learn to read, write, and count the way the white people do. You are also being taught a new religion. You are shown how the white men work and make things. You are living in a new path.

When I was your age, things were entirely different. I had no teacher but my parents and relatives. They are dead and gone now, and I am left alone. It will be the same with you. Your parents are aging and will die some day, leaving you alone. So it is for you to make something of yourselves, and this can only be done while you are young.

In my early days I was eager to learn and do things, and therefore learned quickly, and that made it easier for my teachers. Now I often pick up papers and books which have all kinds of pictures and marks on them, but I cannot understand them as a white person does. They have a way of communicating by the use of written symbols and figures; but before they could do that, they had to have an understanding among themselves. You are learning that, and I was very much pleased to hear you reading.

In future your business dealings with the whites are going to be hard, and it behooves you to learn well what you are taught here. But that is not all. We older people need you. In our dealings with the white man, we are just the same as blind men, because we do not understand them. We need you to help us understand what the white men are up to. My grandchildren, be good. Try and make a mark for yourselves. Learn all you can.

SITTING BULL/TATANKA IYOTAKE
(*Hunkpapa Lakota*), date unknown

6. THE VANISHING INDIAN

Father have pity on me
Father have pity on me
I am crying for thirst
I am crying for thirst
All is gone—I have nothing to eat.

ARAPAHO GHOST DANCE SONG

B Y T H E E N D of the nineteenth century, the general consensus was that the American Indian was a vanishing race, doomed to extinction like the buffalo. They would be pushed toward the setting sun, itself a fitting metaphor for the end of the day of the American Indian. It was not only the non-natives who felt this. Many Native Americans feared the same.

I did not know then
how much was ended.

When I look back
from the high hill of my old age,
I can still see the butchered women and children
lying heaped and scattered
all along the crooked gulch
as plain as when I saw them
with eyes still young.

And I can see that something else
died in that bloody mud,
and was buried in the blizzard.

A people's dream died there.
It was a beautiful dream.

BLACK ELK (*Oglala Lakota*), 1931

In my youthful days, I have seen large herds of buffalo on
these prairies, and elk were found in every grove, but they
are here no more, having gone toward the setting sun. For
hundred of miles no white man lived, but now trading
posts and settlers are found here and there throughout the
country, and in a few years the smoke from their cabins
will be seen to ascend from every grove....

The red man must leave the land of his youth and find
a new home in the west. The armies of the whites are
without number, like the sands of the sea, and ruin will
follow all tribes that go to war with them.

SHABONEE (*Shawnee*), 1827

Sober-thoughted men, far from the scenes of danger, in the
security of cities and populous regions, can talk of "exter-

minating measures," and discuss the policy *of extirpating thousands. . . . In a little while, the remaining tribes will go the way that so many have gone before. The few hordes that still linger about the shores of Huron and Superior, and the tributary streams of the Mississippi, will share the fate of those tribes that once lorded it along the proud banks of the Hudson; of that gigantic race that are said to have existed on the borders of the Susquehanna, and of those various nations, that flourished about the Potomac and the Rappahannock, and that peopled the forests of the vast valley Shenandoah. They will vanish like a vapor from the face of the earth—their very history will be lost in forgetfulness. . . .* WILLIAM APESS *(Pequot),* 1829

In 1830, the U.S. Congress passed the Indian Removal Act, supposedly for the protection of the Indians. It named areas in the West to be "Indian country" in perpetuity, supposedly inaccessible to white settlement. States could now forcibly remove Indians from "non-Indian" land to be relocated west to "Indian country." The best-known story is that of the Cherokee, Choctaw, Seminole, Creek, and Chickasaw, known as the "Five Civilized Tribes" because they adopted many trappings of white civilization in their southern homelands. They had plantations and cattle ranches, published newspapers in their own languages, and ran schools and colleges. The U.S. Supreme Court ruled in favor of the tribes when the Cherokee protested their removal from the homelands.

President Andrew Jackson replied, "The Supreme Court has made their decision, now let them enforce it." The decision was not enforced. The Indian removal that followed was called

Nunna de' ul tsun 'yi in Cherokee, "the place where the people cried." The Trail of Tears. The Cherokee were only one of the many native people forced westward. More than thirty different tribes, from regions in the Northeast, the Southeast, the Midwest, Southwest, and West were exiled to "Indian Territory."

Brother! We have, as your friends, fought by your side, and have poured out our blood in your defense, but our arms are now broken. You have grown large. My people have become small, and there are none who take pity on them.

Brother! My voice is become weak—you can scarcely hear me. It is not the shout of a warrior, but the wail of an infant. I have lost it in mourning over the desolation and injuries of my people. These are their graves which you see scattered around us, and in the winds which pass through these aged pines we hear the moanings of their departed ghosts. Their ashes lie here, and we have been left to protect them. Our warriors are nearly all gone to the west, but here are our dead. Will you compel us to go too, and give up their bones to the wolves? . . .

Brother! You speak the words of a mighty nation. I am a shadow, and scacely reach to your knee. My people are scattered and gone; when I shout, I hear my voice in the depths of the forest, but no answering voice comes back to me—all is silent around me!

COLONEL COBB (*Choctaw*), *circa* 1831

Apache, Arapaho, Caddo, Cayuga, Choctaw, Cherokee, Cheyenne, Chickasaw, Comanche, Creek, Delaware, Iowa, Kaw, Kickapoo, Kiowa, Miami, Missouria, Modoc, Nez Perce,

Osage, Ottawa, Otoe, Pawnee, Peoria, Ponca, Potawatomi, Quapaw, Sac and Fox, Seminole, Seneca, Shawnee, Susquehannock, Tonkawa, Wichita, Wyandotte, and Yuchi all were moved into the Indian Territory (which would become Oklahoma) by the end of the nineteenth century.

> *Friends and relatives—we have reason to glory in the achievements of our ancestors. I behold with sadness the present declining state of our noble race . . . our fathers were strong, and their power was felt and acknowledged far and wide over the American continent. But we have been reduced by the cunning and rapacity of the white-skinned race. We are now compelled to crave, as a blessing, that we may be allowed to live upon our own lands, to cultivate our own fields, to drink from our own springs, and to mingle our bones with those of our fathers. Many winters ago, our wise ancestors predicted that a great monster, with white eyes, would come from the east, and, as he advanced, would consume the land. This monster is the white race, and the prediction is near its fulfilment.*
>
> O - N O - S A *(Seneca), circa* 1848

> *President Jefferson was the first to inaugurate the policy of the removal of the Indians from the States to the country west of the Mississippi. . . . The plan of removal was adopted as the policy of the government, and, by treaty stipulation, affirmed by Congress; lands were set apart for tribes removing into the western wilds, and the faith of a great nation pledged that the homes selected by the Indians should be and remain their homes forever. . . . It is*

presumed that humanity dictated the original policy of the removal and concentration of the Indians in the west to save them from threatened extinction. But to-day, by reason of the immense augmentation of the American population, and the extension of their settlements throughout the entire west, covering both slopes of the Rocky Mountains, the Indian races are more seriously threatened with a speedy extermination than ever before in the history of the country. ELY S. PARKER *(Seneca)*, 1864

Some felt all that would remain would be the romance of their names upon the maps.

My brothers, the Indians must always be remembered in this land. Out of our languages we have given names to many beautiful things which will always speak for us. . . . The broad Iowa and the rolling Dakota and the fertile Michigan will whisper our names to the sun that kisses them. The roaring Niagra, the sighing Illinois, the singing Delaware, will chant unceasingly our death song. Can it be that you and your children will hear the eternal song without a stricken heart. We have been guilty of only one sin—we have had possessions that the white man coveted. We moved away toward the setting sun; we gave up our homes to the white man.

My brethren, among the legends of my people it is told how a chief, leading the remnant of his people, crossed a great river, and striking his tipi-stake upon the ground exclaimed "A-la-ba-ma!" This in our language means "Here we may rest!" But he saw not the future. The white man came: he and his people could not rest there; they were driven out, and in a dark swamp they were thrust down into the slime and killed. The word he so sadly spoke has given a name to one of the white man's states. There is no spot under those stars that now smile upon us, where the Indian can plant his foot and sigh "A-la-ba-ma." It may be that Wakanda will grant us such a place. But it seems that it will only be at His side. WILLIAM J. HARSHA/KHE-THA-A-HI *(Choctaw),* 1881

The Empire State, as you love to call it, was once laced by our trails from Albany to Buffalo—trails that we had trod for centuries—trails worn so deep by the feet of the Iroquois, that they became your roads of travel, as your possessions gradually eat into those of my people. Your roads still traverse those same lines of communication, which bound one part of the Long House to the other. Have we, the first holders of this prosperous region, no longer a share in your history? Glad were your fathers to sit down upon the threshold of the Long House. Had our forefathers spurned you from it, when the French were thundering at the opposite side to get a passage through, and drive you into the sea, whatever has been the fate of other Indians, the Iroquois might still have been a nation, and I, instead of pleading here for the privilege of living within your borders, I—might have had a country.

PETER WILSON *(Cayuga),* 1847

Census figures in 1900 showed a Native American population of the United States of only 237,196. Indian lands continued to diminish. In 1909 alone, President Theodore Roosevelt transferred two and a half million acres of Indian land to the federal government. Indians still did not have full rights as citizens. Even after being granted citizenship in 1924, most Native Americans were not given the right to vote for federal or state offices. They did not have the right to religious freedom. In 1910, the sun dance was made illegal by the U.S. government. Virtually all other traditional religious practices were outlawed as well. The American Indian Freedom of Religion Act would not be passed until 1978.

The problem of European diseases was still a factor in American Indian life—or death—as it had been since the first arrival of Europeans. Epidemics of influenza still swept through with terrifying regularity, and diabetes (brought on by the change in diet forced upon Native Americans) and tuberculosis had become endemic among American Indians. Boarding schools were hotbeds of contagion. Every Indian school had a large graveyard to accommodate the victims of disease. Many young people who came seeking an education instead found an untimely end.

Long ago there were many of us. Before the Americans took our land we lived along the river, up and down and on both sides. Now we have only the reservation. But when I was young my home was in the valley; it is all white people's farms now.

It seems as though you white folks bring poison to us Indians. Sickness comes with you, and hundreds of us die. Where is our strength? Look at me; my father and mother never knew what sickness was, but I, I cough always. In the old times, we were strong. We used to hunt and fish. We raised our little crops of corn and melons and ate the mesquite beans. Now all is changed. We eat the white man's food, and it makes us soft; we wear the white man's heavy clothing and it makes us weak. Each day in the old times in summer and in winter we came down to the river banks to bathe. This strengthened and toughened our firm skins. But white settlers were shocked to see the naked Indians, so now we keep away. In old days we wore the breech-cloth, and aprons made of bark and reeds. We worked all winter in the wind—bare arms, bare legs, and never felt the cold. But now, when the wind blows down from the mountains it makes us cough. Yes—we know that when you come, we die. CHIPAROPAI (Yuma), 1920

All over the American continent, the perception was the same. The American Indian had been reduced in numbers and reduced to a symbol—from once mighty nations to, as the anthropologist Arthur Kroeber subtitled his book about Ishi, the Yahi Indian, "the last of his tribe." The twilight of American Indian life had come. Soon, many believed, that twilight would be followed by an endless night.

We are vanishing from the earth, yet I cannot think we are useless or Usen would not have created us.
GERONIMO/GOYATHLAY (Bedonkohe Apache), 1906

The Wasichus have put us in these square boxes. Our power is gone and we are dying.... But there is another world. BLACK ELK (Oglala Lakota), 1932

What and where would that world be?

I first heard the drum

it was my heart

I first saw the sun

it was the gift

JOSEPH BRUCHAC

7. THE SEVENTH GENERATION

We shall learn all the devices of the white man.

We shall handle his tools for ourselves.

We shall master his machinery, his inventions,

   his skills, his medicine, his planning;

But we'll retain our beauty

And still be Indians!

DAVE MARTINNEZ (Navajo), 1965

AT THE START of the twentieth century it had seemed as if Indians and the Indian way were doomed to extinction. Yet even at that darkest moment, voices were already heralding a new day—just as the old camp criers at dawn would ride through the village calling the people to wake from their slumber. Such white-initiated groups as the Indian Rights Association, organized by the Quakers in 1882, were followed in the twentieth century by new organizations truly Pan-Indian, led by native people themselves.

One of the first of these was the National Congress of American Indians, founded in 1944. Such organizations brought together men and women from many different tribes, some of whom already knew one another—having been sent to the same Indian boarding schools when they were children. Just as Pontiac and Tecumseh did five generations before them, they called together the people to resist a common enemy, this time on battlefields where words and laws were their arrows and their lances.

Gertrude Simmons, a Lakota woman who was published in *The Atlantic Monthly* in 1900 under the name Zitkala-Sa, first gained prominence by telling the Native American story through real Indian eyes. Her literary career, however, was brief. After marrying Raymond T. Bonnin, another Lakota, she devoted most of her energy until her death in 1938 to the cause of American Indian rights and progressive reform, working with such Pan-Indian groups as the Society of the American Indian, and founding the National Council of American Indians. She was a leader in the struggle to gain American citizenship for the American Indian, a fight won at last in 1924.

While still a student at Earlham College in 1896, she argued the right of Native Americans to defend themselves with these words:

What if he fought? His forests were felled; his game frightened away. . . . He loved his family and would defend them. He loved the fair land of which he was rightful owner. He loved the inheritance of his fathers, their traditions, their

groves; he held them a priceless legacy to be sacredly kept.
He loved his native land.

GERTRUDE SIMMONS BONNIN/ZITKALA-SA *(Lakota)*, 1896

Decades later, she would write these words in her article "America's Indian Problem," which predicted the actions that would be taken by the Indians of the twentieth century:

History tells us that it was from the English and the Spanish our government inherited its legal victims, the American Indians, whom to this day we hold as wards and not as citizens of our own freedom loving land. A long century of dishonor followed this inheritance of somebody's loot. Now is the time when the American Indian shall have his day in court through the help of the women of America. The stain upon America's fair name is to be removed, and the remnant of the Indian nation, suffering from malnutrition, is to number among the invited guests at your dinner tables.

GERTRUDE SIMMONS BONNIN/ZITKALA-SA *(Lakota)*, 1900

The native voices of the twentieth century are often so much like those of the centuries past, their appeals to honor and reason so similar, that only the occasional historical reference or turn of phrase distinguishes them. Words spoken two centuries earlier by Red Jacket—who fought on the American side in the War of 1812—are almost identical to those in "An Appeal for Justice," put forward by the Mohawk of the St. Regis Reservation in Hogansburg, New York—many of whom fought in the American armed forces during World War II. The state of New York was about to take land from the few thousand acres remaining to the Iroquois, in violation of treaties signed with the United States.

Many winters ago your forefathers came to our country. They were poor, weak, and feeble. They asked for a little land to plant corn on for their women and children, a place to spread their blankets. We took pity on them. We gave them a great tract of land. Our forefathers taught them how to live in America. They showed them many things: how to plant corn, beans, squashes, potatoes, tomatoes and many more vegetables; showed them how to make sugar from the sap of the maple; told them that the clam and oyster were good to eat; showed them how to make the canoe, the moccasin, the sleeping bag, the snowshoe; they taught them how to smoke the pipe of friendship and peace; taught them healing roots and herbs; showed them the workings, the operation of a great democracy, the Iroquois Government, a system unknown in Europe or Asia. During times of hardship when their little ones cried for bread, it was the Indian who brought them meat, corn and fish.

Now the white man has become strong. Our little countries (Reservations you call them) are all that we have left of this beautiful country, the gift of the Great Spirit to us, his Red Children. We have the right to call this our country. It is ours. We have the written pledge of George Washington that we should have it forever....

A few years ago you won a great war. We fought by

*the side of your generals. We were told that we were fight-
ing for democracy, for the rights of little peoples! Yes, the
blood of our warriors was shed on the battlefields of France,
Germany and Japan for what you then told us was our
common cause, Democracy! Why then, should you wish to
break the sacred agreements between your country and the
Six Nations? Our sacred treaties have been broken like
saplings and your land speculators come forth to cheat and
rob us, your former protector, once a great and powerful
nation, the Iroquois. What harm can our retaining our
reservations and treaties do to you? What are a few thousand acres of land to a great nation like the United
States? ...*

*We want justice from now on. After all that has hap-
pened to us, that is not too much for us to ask. When your
Thirteen Colonies won their freedom from Great Britain
you took a brand from our Council Fire (our government)
and kindled your own fire. Now the same fire is trying to
consume the very people who taught you the worth of such
a fire. . . .*

*The hand that guided and protected your ancestors is
now open to you for justice.*

INDIANS OF THE ST. REGIS RESERVATION *(Mohawk)*, 1948

In the middle of the twentieth century, yet another threat
was posed to tribal survival. The policy called Termination was
begun. Although its stated purpose was to help Indians by re-
moving federal interference, it legislated the termination of
Indian treaty rights and the removal of the government's trust

responsibilities for Indian tribes. The results were tragic. The first tribes whose rights were terminated included, in 1954, the Menominee and the Klamath, tribes that had demonstrated great progress toward self-sufficiency. The settlements given them were pitiful. Upon the signing of the Menominee Termination Act, each member of the former Menominee tribe was given a payment of fifteen hundred dollars, from what had been their own tribal money, and then told that they were on their own. Without federal protection and much-needed benefits long guaranteed by treaties, they were plunged into despair and economic disaster. Unemployment soared. No longer held in common by all of the people of the tribe, much of the land of the former reservations of the Menominee and Klamath people was sold to non-Indians.

In June 1961, a week-long conference was convened at the University of Chicago. The American Indian Chicago Conference, which brought together seven hundred Native Americans representing sixty-four tribes, put forth a Declaration of Indian Purpose.

> *When Indians speak of the continent they yielded, they are not referring only to the loss of some millions of acres in real estate. They have in mind that the land supported a universe of things they knew, valued, and loved.*
>
> *With that continent gone, except for the few poor parcels they still retain, the basis of life is precariously held. . . .*
>
> *In short, the Indians ask for assistance, technical and financial, for the time needed, however long that may be, to regain in the America of the space age some measure of*

the adjustment they enjoyed as the original possessors of their native land.

AMERICAN INDIAN CHICAGO CONFERENCE, 1961

In 1966, Earl Old Person (Blackfeet), testified before Congress against proposed legislation that would have adversely affected Indians. His words were both a summary of the past failures of the United States in dealing with its "Indian problem" and an argument for honoring treaty obligations while allowing Indian self-determination.

In the past 190 years, the U.S. Government has tried every possible way to get rid of the troublesome Indian problem he feels he has on his hands. First the Government tried extinction through destruction—where money was paid for the scalps of every dead Indian. The the Government tried mass relocation and containment through concentration— the moving of entire tribes or parts of tribes to isolated parts of the country where they were herded like animals and fed like animals for the most part. Then the Government tried assimilation—where reservations were broken up into allotments (an ownership system the Indians did not understand) and Indians were forced to try to live like "white men." Indian dances and Indian hand work was forbidden. A family's ration of food was cut off if anyone in the family was caught singing Indian songs or doing Indian hand craft. Children were physically beaten if they were caught speaking Indian languages. Then termination was tried by issuing forced patents in fee to Indian land owners—land was taken out of the trust relationship with the U.S.

*Government and an unrestricted patent in fee was issued
to the Indian whether he wanted it or not or whether he
understood it or not.*

EARL OLD PERSON *(Blackfeet)*, 1966

Led by such people as Earl Old Person and Ada Deer, a
Menominee woman (who would be appointed Director of
Indian Affairs in 1992), native people worked hard to end
termination and restore trust and reservation status. In 1970,
President Richard Nixon announced that "termination is mor-
ally and legally unacceptable, because it produces bad prac-
tical results and because the mere threat of termination tends
to discourage self-sufficiency among Indian groups." In 1973,
Congress passed the Menominee Restoration Act.

*With the passage of the Menominee Termination Act in
1954, a tragic chapter in the tribe's history began. Although designed to free us from federal supervision, termination was a cultural, political and economic disaster.
Our land, our people, and our tribal identity were assailed
in a calculated effort to force us into the mainstream of
society. Like me, other Menominees were wounded to the
heart when, unannounced, bulldozers began slashing and
clearing trees from our beautiful lake shores and slicing
the land into lots to be sold. This was the spark that lit a
fire of determined resistance in us all, resulting in the for-
mation of DRUMS [Determination of Rights and United
for Menominee Shareholders]. DRUMS led a successful
effort to reverse termination, and with the signing of the
Menominee Restoration Act on December 22, 1973, the*

future of the tribe, its land and its people was assured. Working through the legal and political systems, we achieved a historic reversal of an ill-considered and damaging policy, thereby establishing precedents for other tribes in their struggles for self-determination.

Our experience has taught us that despite almost 300 years of disruption, tribal values run deep within each of us. We have two conclusions: first, INDIANS, remain true to your tribal values and traditions; second, the first Americans have a richness and depth of cultures which the world needs, and which our tribes will gladly share.

ADA DEER *(Menominee)*, 1990

Another kind of Indian activism began in the second half of the twentieth century. The sixties were a time of protest, of flower children and hippies, civil rights demonstrations and the Black Panthers. In 1968, the American Indian Law Center was established in Albuquerque, New Mexico. The militant American Indian Movement, AIM, was founded in 1968 in Minneapolis, Minnesota, to promote civil rights for Native Americans.

Although Earl Old Person said in 1966, in his testimony to Congress, that Indians "do not demonstrate in the streets to get our rights," the next few years would prove him wrong. Native American people, fed up with decades of inaction, would turn at last to direct action in November 1969 with the occupation of Alcatraz Island.

According to the 1868 treaty with the Lakota Sioux (a result of Red Cloud's war), any unused federal land was supposed to revert to the Indians. Alcatraz, formerly a federal maximum security prison on an island in San Francisco Bay, had been abandoned in 1963. On November 14, 1969, a group of fourteen American Indian college students occupied Alcatraz. Within a week, more than a hundred Indians were on "the Rock," claiming it as Indian land. They called themselves "Indians of All Tribes." They proposed that Alcatraz should become a Native American university and used Alcatraz as a podium to express Native American grievances about centuries of broken treaties and unfulfilled promises. They maintained control of Alcatraz until June 11, 1971, when they were finally evicted by federal agents. Although Alcatraz would eventually become a part of the national parks system, the effect of the Alcatraz seizure sent ripples through Indian America.

During the stay on Alcatraz, many press releases and documents were produced by the Indians on the island. Some were published in newspapers and magazines. Others ended up in such books as *Alcatraz Is Not an Island,* a volume of essays, photos, and poetry by the Indians of All Tribes. Some who participated in the occupation, such as Native American poets and storytellers Peter Blue Cloud (Mohawk) and Wendy Rose (Hopi/Miwok), would go on to be important figures in the Native American literary renaissance of the 1970s and 1980s. The manifestos from Alcatraz often mixed a deep awareness of history and desire for justice with a typically ironic Indian sense of humor. The following document is one of my favorites. Not only does it mock the language of old treaties, it points out that—even in 1969—Native Americans were still being cheated out of their land or compensated in such ridiculously low amounts as forty-seven cents per acre, which was then being offered to certain California tribes as compensation for land illegally taken in the past.

Proclamation to the Great White Father
and All His People, 1969

We, the native Americans, re-claim the land known as Alcatraz Island in the name of all American Indians by right of discovery.

We wish to be fair and honorable in our dealings with the Caucasian inhabitants of this land, and hereby offer the following treaty:

We will purchase said Alcatraz Island for twenty four dollars (24) in glass beads and red cloth, a precedent set by the white man's purchase of a similar island about 300 years ago. We know that $24 in trade goods for these 16 acres is more than was paid when Manhattan Island was sold, but we know that land values have risen over the years. Our offer of $1.24 per acre is greater than the 47 cents per acre white men are now paying the California Indians for their land. . . .

We feel that this so-called Alcatraz Island is more than suitable for an Indian Reservation, as determined by the white man's own standards. By this we mean that this place resembles most Indian reservations in that:

1. *It is isolated from modern facilities, and without adequate means of transportation.*
2. *It has no fresh running water.*
3. *It has inadequate sanitation facilities.*

4. *There are no oil or mineral rights.*

5. *There is no industry and so unemployment is very great.*

6. *There are no health care facilities.*

7. *The soil is rocky and non-productive; and the land does not support game.*

8. *There are no educational facilities.*

9. *The population has always exceeded the land base.*

10. *The population has always been held as prisoners and kept dependent upon others.*

Further, it would be fitting and symbolic that ships from all over the world, entering the Golden Gate, would first see Indian land, and thus be reminded of the true history of this nation. This tiny island would be a symbol of the great land once ruled by free and noble Indians.

INDIANS OF ALL TRIBES, 1969

Over the next decade, further Indian direct action would include dozens of large-scale marches and demonstrations—much like those that characterized the African American struggle for civil rights. In 1972, Native Americans led a caravan across the continent on the "Trail of Broken Treaties." The trek ended in Washington, D.C., where the offices of the Bureau of Indians Affairs were briefly occupied by Native American demonstrators. In 1973, 200 armed Indians staged a two-month takeover of the Pine Ridge Reservation in South Dakota at Wounded Knee, where a cemetery held the bodies of the Lakota people killed by the U.S. Army in the 1890 massacre of more than 300 Lakota men, women, and children.

These direct actions were matched by successful initiatives in the American courts led by a new generation of Indian lawyers—warriors with briefcases. For the first time, in the second half of the twentieth century, some stolen land was actually returned to Indian nations.

One of the first reparations was to the people of Taos Pueblo in New Mexico. The late nineteenth and earlier twentieth centuries had seen the taking of vast tracts of native lands by the Forest Service to establish multiple-use recreation areas. One such area was Blue Lake, a place of great sacred meaning to the Pueblo. In 1970, a Taos Pueblo delegation presented an appeal to Congress, speaking clearly for a religious freedom which asserted "the profound belief of our people that the trees and all life and the earth itself within the watershed are comparable to human life and must not be cut or injured, but must be protected by wilderness status...." The delegation used the new language of the Native American struggle, a language blending traditional belief with a clear understanding of the process of modern law. No longer would their speeches begin "Brother, ..." Now they would say:

> Mr. Chairman, it has been many years and several congresses since we first came before this subcommittee to appeal for the return of our sacred Blue Lake lands. Our spirits were lifted yesterday as we heard the President of the United States endorse H.R. 471. Like Job in the Biblical story, our people have patiently endured great hardship and deprivation fighting to save the religious heritage embodied in this holy land. In this fight we are also struggling to preserve the identity of our people as a tribe, to

preserve our Indian way of life, and to obtain restitution of land wrongfully taken from us.

We are poor village people, and it has been hard for us to bear the costs of this long struggle for justice over the years since 1906 when the federal government first took the land and put it in the national forest. Even the young children of our village have contributed their pennies to bring our representatives to Washington time and again.

Apart from the financial hardship, we have had to contend with the irreverent curiosity and even mockery that this distasteful, prolonged public conflict has engendered among some white men—such as the threat reported by one of our tribal members in 1968 of a stranger who had declared that he would force his way with a gun into our ceremonies at Blue Lake. That man did not carry out his threat; perhaps because we responded by posting guards to protect our people and the sanctity of their worship. But the incident typifies how difficult it is for everyone—non-Indians as well as Indians—to tolerate the present permit system under which the sacred land is treated on the one hand as an Indian special-use area, on the other as a public multiple-use area.

We ask you to resolve this inherent conflict once and for all by returning the sacred area to our stewardship for religious and traditional use, and by doing so to extend to our people the Constitutional right of all Americans to religious freedom and self-determination. . . .

H.R. 471 . . . would uphold those principles by placing the sacred area under the jurisdiction of the Interior Department in trust for Taos Pueblo—the normal arrange-

ment for Indian lands—and by requiring that it be maintained forever in wilderness status in accordance with the
most fundamental tenets of our religion....

The entire watershed is permeated with holy places and
shrines used regularly by our Indian people; there is no
place that does not have religious significance to us. Each
of the peaks or valleys and lakes, springs, and streams has
a time in our religious calendar when homage in one form
or another must be given, or plants that we have studied
and used for centuries gathered, or rituals performed. Our
religious leaders and societies go regularly to perform these
duties in accordance with this yearly calendar throughout
the area. They also supervise, for a period of eighteen
months, the preparation of our sons for manhood at various
places throughout the sacred area....

All Indians yearn for Congress' recognition of the right
to preserve their cultures, their religion, their tribal governments, and pride in their heritage. We want to take our
rightful place in American society as Indians. Enactment
of H.R. 471 would signal a new policy that will henceforth
support Indian efforts to sustain their culture, their religions, and their tribal governments. Thus, H.R. 471 poses
issues that are national in scope and touch Indians every-
where. We urge you to proclaim such a policy by recom-
mending enactment of H.R. 471.

The past and future of our Indian heritage is in your
hands.   TAOS PUEBLO DELEGATION, 1970

In 1971, Congress passed legislation authorizing the return
of the Blue Lake region to the Taos Pueblo. In 1973, the

Menominee Restoration Act was passed, restoring the relationship between the Menominee nation and the United States, which had been shattered by termination policy. In 1978, the American Indian Freedom of Religion Act was passed, declaring that American Indian religious practices are protected under the First Amendment of the Constitution. And, in 1990, the Native American Languages Act was passed. It stated clearly that "acts of suppression and extermination directed against Native American languages are in conflict with United States policy of self-determination for Native Americans."

Although the goals of true self-determination and the restoration of Native American cultures had not yet been reached, many steps had been taken along that road by the early 1990s. No longer would it be so easy to speak of the vanishing Indian or the inferior status of Native American cultures in an age when more and more Native Americans were speaking out for themselves and their nations. And, as they looked around at the events of the world, Indians would speak not just of their own survival, but of the survival of all. To many in the seventh generation, the voices of the first Americans would be the voices speaking most clearly on behalf of all life.

In 1933, at a time when white scholars were writing about the "Indian problem," Luther Standing Bear spoke for his people.

[There is] no Indian problem as created by the Indian himself. Every problem that exists today in regard to the Indian population is due to the white man's cast of mind. The

white man does not understand the Indian for the reason that he does not understand America. He is too far removed from its formative processes. The roots of the tree of his life have not yet grasped the rock and soil.... But in the Indian the spirit of the land is still vested.

LUTHER STANDING BEAR *(Lakota)*, 1928

More than five decades later, Pam Colorado wrote on the idea of "Native science," a science based not just on contemporary Western ideas but on the Native American ways of experiencing and interacting with the natural world.

Indian science, often understood through the tree, is holistic. Through spiritual processes, it synthesizes or gathers information from the mental, physical, social, cultural, and historical realms. Like a tree, the roots of Native science go deep into the history, body, and blood of the land. The tree collects, stores, and exchanges energy.... Why, how the trees does this is a mystery, but the Indian observes the tree to emulate, complement and understand his/her relationship to this beautiful, life-enhancing process.... Seeking truth and coming to knowledge necessitates studying the cycles, relationships, and connections between things. Indeed, a law of Native science requires that we look ahead seven generations when making decisions!

From South America to the Arctic, the tree and all that it implies has been guiding and shaping the thought of Native peoples since the dawn of humanity. Those who follow this natural science do so in search of balance, harmony or peace with all living relations. Iroquois call this Skanagoah.

Skanagoah, literally interpreted as "great peace," is the term used to describe the still, electrifying awareness one experiences in the deep woods. This feeling or state of balance is at the heart of the universe and is the spirit of Native science. PAM COLORADO *(Oneida)*, 1988

In 1992, at a conference bringing together Native American writers from the four corners of North America, one of the main topics of concern was earth and the circle of life. The words of Linda Hogan and Harold Littlebird were spoken not only for the present, but for the generations before us and those yet to come.

We had a pact, a sacred trust with the land that was thousands of years old, before European presence on this continent. We had complex systems of agriculture and tradition and religion, and knowledge about what is now called ecology.

We're all wounded, not just Indian people, but all of us have been wounded by the culture that has split us from the natural world, from our inner lives, and from our dreams. When we were broken as people, so was the bond between us and the land, the sacred agreement that we had. Not many years after colonization, after what is sometimes called exploration, but what we call conquest, the environment was already severely affected. So what is happening to the environment isn't just happening now, it's been happening all along.

In 1978, the Religious Freedoms Act was passed. Most non-Indian people don't realize that in 1894, all Indian religions were banned by the Bureau of Indian Affairs in the United States. So it was illegal for us to practice our own traditions until 1978, and there were people incarcerated for practicing traditional religions. The Freedom of Religion Act really focuses a great deal on land issues, on sacred sites, on the destruction of sacred sites. We're the only people whose religion has ties to the land in this country.

Sacred is an interesting word to think about what the meaning of it is. I heard someone once define sacred as that which could be destroyed but could not be created. I think it's important to look at that when we're thinking about what has happened to the land and the treaties that have been broken that had to do with land and a different concept of ownership. Being owned by the land is how Native people see it. . . .

LINDA HOGAN *(Chickasaw),* 1992

We know we can still hold on to those things because we know we all come from story. We know we all come from places of emergence. They may not all be the same story but there is a sameness. There is a oneness in it all and it comes from language. It comes from places where the word was sacred, and is sacred, and will remain sacred.

HAROLD LITTLEBIRD *(Laguna/Santo Domingo Pueblo),* 1992

Perhaps it can be said that to truly understand this land, and to preserve it for the generations to come, we all must begin to see it through Indian eyes. A Mohawk elder named Tom Porter told me in 1990 that there was an old prophecy he had never understood until recently. That prophecy is this: "One day our children will speak to the world."

Today, as the seventh generation speaks to the world, we may be closer to that time when both Native American people and this land will be respected and understood.

The story of American Indian people does not end here. And it is not just a story about those whose ancestors first knew and cared for this land. As I look around me, seeing with Indian eyes, I do so with pride. I recognize how much of the world we live in has been shaped by Native American culture and Native American contributions. The equality of women, ideas of participatory democracy, foods that we eat, words that we speak, the names on the land around us all have roots that may be traced back to American Indian nations. The United States is a land that has been deeply influenced by its first peoples.

And that influence has not ended. On the one hand, contemporary Native American men and women work in every walk of American life, from science to labor, from national politics to the military, from education to the arts. Sometimes those contributions are made quietly, as American Indians work side by side with and indistinguishable from other Americans.

In other cases, the distinctiveness of native culture itself has been part of their contribution. During World War II, Navajo soldiers helped devise a secret code, using their own language, which was used to transmit crucial information during the Pacific campaign. Every other American military code was broken except for the one used by the Navajo Code Talkers. Ironically, those same Navajo men, while students in government Indian schools, had been forbidden to speak their own language. New generations of Native American artists and writers have achieved worldwide recognition as they've interpreted and shared their Native American heritage through paintings and sculpture, poetry and fiction.

If America has accepted much that is American Indian, sometimes without even recognizing that a contribution has been made from Native American people, there is also much that remains to be heard from the American Indian, much that could still be learned from nations that sought to live in physical and spiritual equilibrium with all life. The "new" ideas of ecology are ancient practice for Native Americans.

Listen to the voices of seven generations. Know that these voices are also the voices of the land, with lasting echoes. For the sake of seven generations to come, listen closely and try to understand.

When I first heard the drum,
I did not yet know
that it was my heart
and the heart of my mother.

When I first saw the sun,
I could not see
that it was the gift
of life from our Creator.

The stories helped me
to understand.

The words of elders led me
to walk with care
on this land.

An old song says
Earth always remains.
Beneath our feet
the earth is alive.

If we stay close to the earth
and do not forget,
we, too, may survive.

The lives and words
of our ancestors
are part of the land,
lasting echoes, never gone.

They return to us
with each story, each song,
as old as the sun,
as new as each dawn.

JOSEPH BRUCHAC (*Abenaki*), 1997

FOR FURTHER READING

For further information about the lives of American Indians and for a deeper understanding of the chronology and history of native America, I recommend the following books. Some are by native and some by non-native authors, but all of them quote extensively from American Indians and approach their subject with great sympathy for the Native American viewpoint.

Champagne, Duane, editor. *Native America: Portrait of the Peoples.* Detroit: Visible Ink Press, 1994.

Francis, Lee (Laguna Pueblo). *Native Time: A Historical Time Line of Native America.* New York: St. Martin's Press, 1996.

Hamilton, Charles, editor. *Cry of the Thunderbird: The American Indian's Own Story.* Norman, Oklahoma: University of Oklahoma Press, 1972.

Harvey, Karen D., and Lisa D. Harjo (Choctaw). *Indian Country: A History of Native People in America.* Golden, Colorado: North American Press, 1994.

Hirschfelder, Arlene, and Martha Krepe De Montaäno. *The Native American Almanac: A Portrait of Native America Today.* New York: Prentice Hall General Reference, 1993.

Miller, Lee, editor (Cherokee/Kaw). *From the Heart: Voices of the American Indian.* New York: Alfred A. Knopf, 1995.

Nies, Judith. *Native American History: A Chronology of the Vast Achievements of a Culture and Their Links to World Events.* New York: Ballantine Books, 1996.

Vanderwerth, W. C., compiler. *Indian Oratory: Famous Speeches by Noted Indian Chieftains*. Norman, Oklahoma: University of Oklahoma Press, 1971.

Eagle Walking Turtle (Choctaw). *Indian America: A Traveler's Companion*. Santa Fe, New Mexico: John Muir Publications, 1995.

TRIBAL AFFILIATIONS AND LIFETIMES

A listing of tribal affiliations and dates for some of the most prominent Native Americans quoted in this book follows. Because Native American people in the past did not keep chronological records in the same way Europeans did, information such as exact birth dates is sometimes impossible to pinpoint. In some cases, as with William Apess, there may not even be a record of the individual's death. As much as possible, I have gone with what the individuals said about themselves, and I have included both their English names and their names in the Native language.

Native people still refer to themselves as American Indians, although contemporary reference is Native American. I have used these terms interchangeably in this book to reflect how they are used today. *(References to text pages follow each entry.)*

William Apess (Pequot) 1798–18?
 pp. 32, 77–79, 100–101
Black Elk (Oglala Lakota) 1863–1950
 pp. 99–100, 107
Black Hawk/Makataimeshekiakiak (Mesquakie) 1767–1838
 pp. 26, 33
Gertrude Simmons Bonnin/Zitkala-Sa (Lakota) 1876–1938
 pp. 110–11
Chief Joseph/In-mut-too-yah-lat-lat (Nez Perce) 1840–1904
 pp. 55–56, 65–68

SOURCES FOR QUOTATIONS

(1691) by Father Christian LeClercq. Translated by William F. Ganong. Toronto: The Champlain Society, 1910.

5–6 Cheyenne Ghost Dance Song, circa 1890.

8 Maungwaduaus (Ojibway). From *History of the Ojebway Indians* by Chief Kahkewaquonaby Peter Jones. London: n.p., 1861.

8–9 Zuni Sunrise Prayer. Collected by Ruth Bunzel in "Zuni Origin Myths." Bureau of American Ethnology Report. Washington, D.C., 1933.

9–10 Carl Sweezy (Arapaho). From *The Arapaho Way: A Memoir of an Indian Boyhood* by Althea Bass. New York: Crown Publishers, 1996.

11 Iroquois speaker (unnamed). From *The History of the Five Nations of Canada* by Cadwallader Colden. London: n.p., 1755.

12–13 Red Jacket/Sagoyewatha (Seneca). (Spoken to U.S. Senate on March 26, 1792.) From *The Life and Times of Sa-Go-Ye-Wat-Ha, or Red Jacket* by William L. Stone. New York: Wiley & Putnam, 1841.

CHAPTER 2

15 Pawnee Song to the Sky. Collected by Frances Densmore in "Pawnee Music." Bureau of American Ethnology Report. Washington, D.C., 1929.

17 Wahunsenacawh (Powhatan). From *Lives of Celebrated American Indians* by Samuel Griswold Goodrich. Boston: Bradbury, Sooden, 1843.

18–19 Otreouti (Iroquois). (Spoken to the French governor.) From *Indian Biography* by B. B. Thatcher. New York: J & J Harper & Bros., 1822.

20 Iroquois Faith Keeper. (Spoken as a Thanksgiving address.) From *League of the Ho-de-no-sau-nee, Iroquois* by Lewis H. Morgan. Rochester: Sage & Brothers, 1851.

21 Smohalla (Wanapam). From Bureau of American Ethnology Report, Part II. Washington, D.C., 1896.

21 Georgetta Stonefish Ryan. From the National Museum of the American Indian brochure, 1992.

22 Miantonomi (Narragansett). From *Biography and History of the Indians of North America* by Samuel Drake. Boston: Antiquarian Institute, 1837.

22 Canassatego (Seneca). From *Indian Treaties Printed by Benjamin Franklin, 1736–1762*, edited by Julian P. Boyd. Philadelphia: Historical Society of Pennsylvania, 1938.

22 Minavavana (Chippewa). From *Indian Biography* by B. B. Thatcher. New York: J & J Harper & Bros., 1841.

23–24 Chief Gieschenatsi/Hard Man (Shawnee). From *The Life and Times of David Zeisberger: The Western Pioneer and Apostle of the Indians* by Edmund de Schweinitz. Philadelphia: J. B. Lippincott, 1870.

24–25 Chief Gieschenatsi/Hard Man (Shawnee). From *Wampum Belts and Peace Trees* by Gregory Schaaf. Golden, Colo.: Fulcrum Publishing, 1990.

25 Speckled Snake (Creek). From *Niles Weekly Register,* 20 June 1829.

26 Black Hawk/Makataimeshekiakiak (Mesquakie). From *The Sauks and the Black Hawk War* by Perry S. Armstrong. Springfield, Ill.: H. W. Rokker, 1887.

27 Satanta (Kiowa). From the *New York Times*, 20 November 1867.

27–28 Ten Bears (Comanche). From Proceedings of the Indian Peace Commission, Volume 2, Record Group No. 48., Washington, D.C.: National Archives, 1867.

28–29 Sitting Bull/Tatanka Iyotake (Hunkpapa Lakota). From the *Chicago Tribune*, 5 July 1879.

CHAPTER 3

31 Cherokee Charm for Protection and Success in Battle. From *The Shadow of Sequoyah, Social Documents of the Cherokee, 1862–1964* by Jack F. and Anna G. Kilpatrick. Norman: University of Oklahoma Press, 1964.

32 From "Eulogy on King Philip" by William Apess. Boston: n.p., 1836.

33 Black Hawk/Makataimeshekiakiak (Mesquakie). From *Life of Ma-ka-tai-me-she-kia-kiak or Black Hawk, Dictated by Himself.* Boston: n.p., 1834.

34 Sir Jeffrey Amherst, Commander of the British forces. From *The Conspiracy of Pontiac* by Frances Parkman. Boston: Little, Brown, 1913.

34–35 From *History of the Ottawa and Chippewa Indians of Michigan* by Chief Andrew J. Blackbird. Ypsilanti, Mich.: n.p., 1887.

35 Ojibway Song to the Buffalo. Adapted from "Poems from Sioux and Chippewa Songs," collected by Frances Densmore. Bureau of American Ethnology Report. Washington, D.C., 1917.

35 Assiniboine Warrior's Prayer. Adapted from "Indian Tribes of the Upper Missouri" by Edwin T. Denig. Bureau of American Ethnology Report. Washington, D.C., 1930.

38–40 Pontiac (Ottawa). (Spoken on April 27, 1763, before his attack on Detroit.) From *The Conspiracy of Pontiac, Volume I* by Francis Parkman. Champlain Editions, 1898.

40 Pontiac (Ottawa). (Spoken on May 23, 1763.) From *Indian Biography* by B. B. Thatcher. New York: J & J Harper & Bros., 1832.

41 Cornstalk (Shawnee). From *Old Frontiers* by John P. Brown. Arno Press, 1971.

41 Captain Pipe/Hopocan (Delaware). From Thatcher, 1832.

42–43 Tecumseh (Shawnee). From *Biography and History of the Indians of North America* by Samuel Drake. Boston: Antiquarian Institute, 1837.

44 Tecumseh (Shawnee). From *History of the Choctaw, Chickasaw, and Natchez Indians* by Horace Bardwell Cushman. Greenville, Texas: Headlight Printing House, 1899.

44–45 Pushmataha (Choctaw). From *Memorial Services at the Grave of Pushmataha.* Congressional Record, 13 June 1921.

45–46 Tecumseh (Shawnee). From *War of 1812* by Major John Richardson. Brockville: Ontario-Canada West, 1842.

46 Teton Sioux Song. Collected by Frances Densmore in "Teton Sioux Music." Bureau of American Ethnology Report. Washington, D.C., 1918.

46 Wants-to-Die (Crow). (Before joining a war party.) From "The Religion of the Crow Indians" by Robert H. Lowie. Anthropological Papers of the American Museum of Natural History, Vol. 25. New York, 1922.

47–48 Red Iron (Sisseton Dakota). From *A Century of Dishonor* by Helen Jackson Hunt. Boston: n.p., 1893.

48 Little Crow/Taoyeduta (Santee Dakota). From "As Red Men Viewed It: Three Accounts of the Uprising," edited by Kenneth Carley. *Minnesota History* 38, 1962.

49 General Philip Sheridan. From *The Great Buffalo Hunt* by Wayne Gard. New York: Alfred A. Knopf, 1959.

50 Sitting Bear/Satank (Kiowa). From *Austin (Texas) Triweekly Republican.* 17 December 1867.

50–51 Chief Little Robe (Cheyenne.) From *The Hunting of the Buffalo* by Douglas E. Branch. New York: D. Appleton & Co., 1929.

51 Striking Eagle (Kiowa). From *The Buffalo War* by James L. Haley. New York: Doubleday, 1976.

52 Sitting Bull/Tatanka Iyotake (Hunkpapa Lakota). From *Forty Years as a Fur Trader on the Upper Missouri, 1833–1872,* edited by Milo M. Quaife. Chicago: Lakeside Classics, 1933.

52 Sitting Bull/Tatanka Iyotake (Hunkpapa Lakota). From *On the Great Highway: The Wanderings and Adventures of a Special Correspondent* by James Creelman. Boston: Lothrop Publishing Co., 1901.

53 Havasupai Prayer. Adapted from *Havasupai Ethnography* by Leslie Spier, Anthropological Papers of the American Museum of Natural History, Vol. 29. New York, 1928.

CHAPTER 4

55 Osage War Song. From *War Ceremony and Peace Ceremony of the Osage Indians* by Francis LaFlesche. Bureau of American Ethnology Report. Washington, D.C., 1939.

56 Chief Joseph/In-mut-too-yah-lat-lat (Nez Perce). From 45th Congress, 2nd Session, House Executive Document I, 1877.

57 Half Town, Cornplanter, and Big Tree (Seneca). From *Biography and History of the Indians of North America* by Samuel Drake. Boston: Antiquarian Institute, 1837.

57–58 Red Jacket/Sagoyewatha (Seneca). From *Biography and History of the Indians of North America* by Samuel Drake. Boston: B. S. Mussey & Co., 1848.

58–59 William Weatherford/Red Eagle (Creek). From *Adventures among the Indians* by W. H. G. Kingston. Chicago: n.p., prior to 1850.

59 Last Song of Sitting Bull. Collected by Frances Densmore in "Teton Sioux Music." Bureau of American Ethnology Report. Washington, D.C., 1918.

60 Red Cloud (Lakota). From the *New York Times*, 17 July 1870.

61–62 Cochise (Chiracahua Apache). From Kansas State Historical Society Collections, Vol. 13.

64 Sitting Bull/Tatanka Iyotake (Hunkpapa Lakota). From *Life of Sitting Bull and History of the War of 1890–91* by W. Fletcher Johnson. New York: Edgewood Publishing Co., 1891.

64–65 Sitting Bull/Tatanka Iyotake (Hunkpapa Lakota). From Johnson, 1891.

65–66 Chief Joseph/In-mut-too-yah-lat-lat (Nez Perce). From "An Indian's View of Indian Affairs," *The North American Review*, April 1879.

66 Chief Joseph/In-mut-too-yah-lat-lat (Nez Perce). From *The North American Review*, April 1879.

66–68 Chief Joseph/In-mut-too-yah-lat-lat (Nez Perce). From *The North American Review*, April 1879.

69 Geronimo/Goyathlay (Bedonkohe Apache). Reprinted in *The Truth about Geronimo* by Britten Davis. New Haven: Yale University Press, 1929.

CHAPTER 5

71 Little Raven (Arapaho). (Spoken June 1871 at Cooper Union.) From *Report of Commissioner of Indian Affairs.* Washington, D.C.: U.S. Government Printing Office, 1871.

72–73 Unidentified Iroquois. From *Biography and History of the Indians of North America* by Samuel Drake. Boston: Antiquarian Institute, 1837.

75 Samson Occom (Mohegan). From *Samson Occom's Journals.* Volumes 1–3. Hanover, N.H.: Dartmouth College Archives.

75–76 Samson Occom (Mohegan). From *Samson Occom's Journals.*

77 Samson Occom (Mohegan). From *Samson Occom's Journals.*

79 William Apess (Pequot). From *A Son of the Forest.* New York: n.p., 1829.

82–83 Sarah Winnemucca (Paiute). From *Life among the Piutes.* New York: Putnam, 1883.

84 Sarah Winnemucca (Paiute). From *Life among the Piutes.*

85 Sarah Winnemucca (Paiute). From *Life among the Piutes.*

86 Sarah Winnemucca (Paiute). From the *Daily Alta California,* 1883.

87 Unidentified Navajo students at the Tohatchi School, New Mexico. From "Indians at Work," U.S. Government publication, 1933. Reprinted in *Rising Voices,* edited by Arlene Hirschfelder and Beverly Singer. New York: Macmillan, 1992.

87–88 Chiparopai (Yuma). From *The Indians' Book* by Natalie Curtis. New York: Harper and Bros., 1923.

88–89 Luther Standing Bear (Lakota). From *My People the Sioux.* Boston: Houghton Mifflin, 1928. Reprinted, Lincoln: University of Nebraska Press, 1975.

90 Unidentified Santa Fe woman (Santa Clara). From *One House, One Voice, One Heart: Native American Education at the Santa Fe Indian School* by Sally Hyer. Santa Fe, N.M.: Museum of New Mexico Press, 1990.

91 Unidentified boy (Apache). From Hyer, 1990.

92 Mountain Wolf Woman (Winnebago). From *Mountain Wolf Woman,* edited by Nancy Oestreich Lurtie. Ann Arbor: University of Michigan Press, 1961.

93 Quanah Parker (Comanche). From words recorded at a council on reservation use, June 1881. Reprinted in *Quanah Parker, Comanche*

Chief by William T. Hagan. Norman: University of Oklahoma Press, 1996.

93 Quanah Parker (Comanche). From a letter written to the Indian agent expressing his opposition to his people participating in the Ghost Dance, 1890. From Hagan, 1996.

93–94 Quanah Parker (Comanche). From a letter to the Commissioner of Indian Affairs after visit with and advising the Mescalero Apache in New Mexico, 1892. From Hagan, 1996.

94 Quanah Parker (Comanche). Spoken at a meeting at Fort Sill to discuss the sale of Comanche lands after the Dawes Allotment Act, which required the breaking up of Indian lands held in common in Oklahoma, the allotment of 160 acres to each Indian, and the opening of the remaining lands to white homesteaders, September 1892. From Hagan, 1996.

94 Quanah Parker (Comanche). Spoken at a council, 1895. From Hagan, 1996.

94 Quanah Parker (Comanche). Letter to Theodore Roosevelt regarding the return of a herd of buffalo to the Wichita National Game Preserve, 1907. From Hagan, 1996.

95 Quanah Parker (Comanche), 1896. From Hagan, 1996.

96–97 Sitting Bull/Tatanka Iyotake (Hunkpapa Lakota). From *Warpath and Council Fire* by Stanley Vestal. Norman: University of Oklahoma Press, 1949.

CHAPTER 6

99 Arapaho Ghost Dance Song. From *The Ghost-Dance Religion and the Sioux Outbreak of 1890* by James Mooney.

99–100 Black Elk (Oglala Lakota). From *Black Elk Speaks*, edited by John G. Neihardt. New York: William Morrow, 1932. Reprinted, Lincoln: University of Nebraska Press, 1961.

100 Shabonee (Shawnee). From *The American Indian* 2, no. 8 (1928).

100–101 William Apess (Pequot). From *A Son of the Forest*. New York: n.p., 1829.

102 Colonel Cobb (Choctaw). From *Documents and Official Reports Illustrating the Causes Which Led to the Revolution in the Government of the Seneca Indians*. Baltimore: W. M. Woody & Son, 1857.

103 O-no-Sa (Seneca). From *League of the Ho-de-no-sau-nee, or Iroquois* by Lewis Henry Morgan. Rochester, N.Y.: Sage & Brothers, 1851.

103–104 Ely S. Parker (Seneca). From Senate Executive Document No. 13, 40th Congress, 1st Session, 24 January 1864.

104–105 William J. Harsha/Khe-tha-a-hi (Choctaw). From *Ploughed Under: The Story of an Indian Chief Told by Himself.* Self-published, 1881.

105 Peter Wilson (Cayuga). From *League of the Ho-de-no-sau-nee, or Iroquois* by Lewis Henry Morgan. Rochester, N.Y.: Sage & Brothers, 1851.

106–107 Chiparopai (Yuma). From *The Indians' Book* by Natalie Curtis. New York: Harper and Bros., 1923.

107 Geronimo/Goyathlay (Bedonkohe Apache). From *Geronimo's Story of His Life,* as told to and edited by S. M. Barrett. New York: Duffield, 1906.

107 Black Elk (Oglala Lakota). From *Black Elk Speaks.* Reprinted, 1961.

CHAPTER 7

109 Dave MartinNez (Navajo). From *Anthology of Poetry and Verse.* Washington, D.C.: Bureau of Indian Affairs, 1965.

110–111 Gertrude Simmons Bonnin/Zitkala-Sa (Lakota). From *The Earlhamite.* Earlham, Iowa: Earlham College, 16 March 1896.

111 Gertrude Simmons Bonnin/Zitkala-Sa (Lakota). From "America's Indian Problem," *The Atlantic Monthly,* January 1990.

112–13 Indians of the St. Regis Reservation (Mohawk). From *The American Indian* 4, no. 3 (1948).

114–15 American Indian Conference. From *Declaration of Purpose.* Chicago, 1961.

115–16 Earl Old Person (Blackfeet). From The Congressional Record, 1961.

116–17 Ada Deer (Menominee). From *After Columbus: The Smithsonian Chronicle of the North American Indian* by A. J. Viola. Washington, D.C.: Smithsonian/Orion Books, 1990.

119–20 Indians of All Tribes, 1969.

121–23 Taos Pueblo Delegation. From The Congressional Record, 91st Congress, 2nd Session, 1970.

124–25 Luther Standing Bear (Lakota). From his *My People the Sioux.* Boston: Houghton Mifflin, 1928.

125–26 Pam Colorado (Oneida). From *New Voices from the Longhouse,* edited by Joseph Bruchac. Greenfield Center, N.Y.: Greenfield Review Press, 1989.

126–27 Linda Hogan (Chickasaw). From *Reclaiming the Vision: Past, Present, and Future Native Votes for the Eighth Generation* by James Bruchac and Lee Francis, 1996.

127 Harold Littlebird (Laguna/Santo Domingo Pueblo). From Bruchac and Francis, 1996.

Acknowledgments

We gratefully acknowledge the following for permission to reprint from previously published material:

Beyond Words Publishing, Inc. (1-800-284-9673). From *Wisdomkeepers: Meetings with Native American Spiritual Elders.* Copyright © 1990 by Steve Wall and Harvey Arden.

Crown Publishers, Inc. From *The Arapaho Way: A Memoir of an Indian Boyhood* by Althea Bass. Copyright © 1996 by Mrs. John Harvey Bass.

Fulcrum Publishing. From *Wampum Belts and Peace Trees: George Morgan, Native Americans, and Revolutionary Diplomacy.* Copyright © 1990 by Gregory Schaaf.

Greenfield Review Press. From *Reclaiming the Vision: Past, Present and Future Native Voices for the Eighth Generation.* Copyright © 1996 by James Bruchac and Lee Francis. Reprinted by permission of the editors. From *New Voices from the Longhouse: An Anthology of Contemporary Iroquois Writing.* Copyright © 1989 by Joseph Bruchac. Reprinted by permission of the editor.

The Museum of New Mexico Press. From *One House, One Voice, One Heart: Native American Education at the Santa Fe Indian School* by Sally Hyer. Copyright © 1990 by Santa Fe Indian School.

Orion Books/Crown Publishers. From *After Columbus: The Smithsonian Chronicle of the North American Indians.* Copyright © 1990 by Herman J. Viola.